Ex Libris

Randy Henning

CROP CIRCLES

CONCLUSIVE EVIDENCE?

CROP CIRCLES

CONCLUSIVE EVIDENCE?

PAT
DELGADO

BLOOMSBURY

First published in Great
Britain 1992
Bloomsbury Publishing
Limited, 2 Soho Square,
London W1V 5DE

PICTURE SOURCES

Colin Andrews: pages 72, 97
Stuart and Julie Baker: pages
53, 64, 69, 70, 71, 90-1, 92,
94
Mrs G. Bell: page 19
Cambridge Newspapers
Limited: pages 110-11
Doug Cooper: page 130
Chad Deetkin: pages 60, 61,
62, 62-3, 68
'Diane': pages 140, 141, 143,
144
Nathan Elliot: page 35
European Press Association:
page 133
Grimsby Evening Telegraph:
page 93
Tony James: pages 43, 48
Ann Jones: pages 131, 132
Dr and Mrs King: pages 75,
118

Dr W. C. Levengood: pages
152, 153
Sid Moss: page 55
Steve Patterson: pages 44-5,
50-1
A.P. Railton: page 74
Gary Rose: pages 49, 52
Helmut Schäffer: page 76
South Coast Photographics:
page 40
Richard Tarr: page 22
A. Trapnell: page 23
Matthew Whitehall: pages 40-1

All other photographs taken
by Pat Delgado

A CIP catalogue record for
this book is available from the
British Library

ISBN 0–7475–1282–5

10 9 8 7 6 5 4 3 2 1

Designed by Bradbury and
Williams
Typeset by Florencetype Ltd,
Kewstoke, Avon
Printed by Butler & Tanner
Ltd, Frome and London

We are all too much inclined, I think, to walk through life with our eyes closed. There are things around us and right at our very feet that we have never seen, because we have never really looked. We should not keep forever on the public road going only where others have gone; we should leave the beaten track occasionally and enter the woods. Every time you do that you will be certain to find something you have never seen before. Of course, it will be a little thing; but do not ignore it. Follow it up, explore all round it; one discovery will lead to another and before you know it you will have something worth thinking about to occupy your mind, for all really big discoveries are the results of thought.

Alexander Graham Bell

ACKNOWLEDGEMENTS

My sincere thanks to all those who alerted me to the appearance of various crop circles and patterns, and to all those named in this book who have contributed to its production. My thanks also to the landowners and farmers who allowed me on to their land.

My gratitude to my wife, Norah, for her help and her tolerance of my long periods of absence while I was gathering material, and to my daughter, Jan, for accompanying me on many field trips and photographic flights and for her unflagging interest and hard work in assisting with this book.

Contents

INTRODUCTION

This is a book about the mysterious flattened swirled crop circles and pictograms in which I ask you to assess the evidence I place before you. It follows the two books written by Colin Andrews and myself, *Circular Evidence* and *Crop Circles: The Latest Evidence*. It was the ceaseless clamour for more information which prompted me to write a third book, this time without Colin, as he is extremely busy with other projects associated with the subject.

In this book, as in the others, I have included many photographs, the majority to accompany the descriptions of the crop circles and pictograms of 1991. Visual impact is a major source of pleasure in studying crop circles and once you have seen the contents of this book I am sure you will agree with me. The ever-increasing complexity of the patterns took a huge leap forward when the Mandelbrot Set appeared near Cambridge. This was indeed a bonus after Barbury Castle, which at the time we thought could not be surpassed. Just what a Mandelbrot Set is and what its implications are for the subject is discussed in detail.

Keeping records and photographs of the subject is only a part of the research that is going on. Crop analysis has produced interesting results, as has surveillance, all of which are revealed. Of course, these are all tangible aspects of the subject and, as anyone who knows anything about crop circles

knows, many bizarre things can happen. I have written about some of them, and in particular the one at Highland in Kansas, USA – still as big a mystery today as the day it happened.

I also suggest how crop circles affect us spiritually, and discuss the symbolism that lies within, and affinity we have with, them.

Finally, I am indebted to many people for their help in reporting and photographing many circle sites both in the UK and overseas. Indeed, without their help and enthusiasm much of this book might not have been written.

The evidence is within. The decision is yours.

THE EVOLUTION IN 1991

It was with great expectancy that we entered the 1991 season, hoping there was going to be a spectacular leap forward in the presentation of crop pictograms. We were not disappointed.

The year started reasonably quietly with the first activity in late April and early May. It was the single circle at Butleigh Wootton that created the first buzz of excitement, and there were many stories and much speculation about its validity.

The dust from that event had hardly settled when about two weeks later the next event was reported. It was announced over the communications network that a pattern had been seen in a crop of oil-seed rape somewhere west of Warminster in Wiltshire. Apparently the site was being kept secret to protect the field from invasion by visitors. It was eventually located alongside the A303 at Yarnbury Castle. The pattern was a dumb-bell shape, so here was an immediate advance this year beyond the single circle. The speculation this time was about the complexity of the pattern and whether this was an indication of bigger things to come.

This event was followed by two reports of circles, one at Newquay in Cornwall and the other at Urchfont in Wiltshire. Both of these were quickly written off as obvious hoaxes. These events were seen as a minor set-back. Hoaxing is a source of irritation and a waste of time. The day was saved by the

appearance of a precise single circle in a field on the Isle of Wight. A report follows later (see page 15).

The next features to be found were at Pepperbox Hill, south of Salisbury. The patterns here were well advanced, with their assortment of circles, corridors and boxes. They were such a large step forward in design for this year that a question mark has hung over them for a few researchers. Others considered it was reasonable to accept them. The patterns could be related to many of those seen in 1990. After all, we were expecting something exciting and these offered a step in the right direction. Even the crop stems' rate of recovery to the vertical was acceptable at this stage of growth. So there they were, in the last week of May: the most intricate designs this year.

Reports of circles and pictograms came in almost every other day in June and I was surprised at the number considered to be the work of pranksters. They all had to be recorded so that their location was known for repetitive reports.

It was not until the first week in July that Richard Tarr's report deviated from the succession of single-circle and small-formation reports. He described a long pictogram at Newton St Loe in Avon, and as the photographs show, it took its place with those in the 1990 Alton Barnes category but with subtle differences. It achieved the distinction of drawing level with the complexity of the 1990 pictograms but, even so, there was still an atmosphere of waiting for something really spectacular.

This is where we arrive at a crucial factor in the crop-circle phenomenon, for what has been highlighted now is the undeniable clamour for bigger and better showpieces in the fields. It is an inevitable result of human nature that design repetition in pictograms results in loss of impact. There is almost a requirement for continuous improvement, and so that we are not disillusioned we are given fresh hope and expectancy at intervals by the arrival of a new and dramatic event.

If pictogram evolution was drawn on a graph we would see a line steadily increasing in height but with sharp peaks. These are the interest boosters, which assist our ideas to evolve along with the phenomenon. I wonder how many people would fall by the wayside if there were no such boosters and we only had single circles to study.

Throughout July there were plenty of variations and combinations of patterns made up of circles and central corridors. This was the evolution of the dumb-bell. A further stage occurred during August, when there was an exhibition of various point-ended ellipses with these extremities surrounded by rings. The bodies of these ellipses ranged from small to large and from narrow to wide, and when photographs of them are grouped together it is clear that there are not many variations left. That stage of the evolution had come to its end.

Of course, the highlights of the year were the sensational Barbury Castle pictogram and the Ickleton Mandelbrot Set. There is no way of knowing what form the evolutionary curve will take, or if it will revert back to the beginning, with just plain single circles for us to ponder. Or does the power of the human mind demand or dictate the progress of crop pictograms? We have an insatiable desire to understand the unknown. Whatever the case, there is no turning back, like the thriller you cannot put down until the plot has run its course or the culprit is exposed. Until it is intended to do so, there will be no bursting of the evolutionary bubble of the crop-circle phenomenon.

BUTLEIGH WOOTTON
near Glastonbury, Avon

This was the first crop circle of the 'season'. We first heard about it through the network of observers, that great band of people who are forever looking out over the fields for signs that something unusual has occurred.

It was 20 April when Colin and I drove along the scenic country roads to the site, noting that Glastonbury Tor was only about three miles to the north. We spotted the single circle in the corner of a field and close to a crossroads which we had just reached. After parking the car we climbed a convenient earth mound to get a better view and I also took some photographs with the camera on a pole. We wanted the farmer's permission to go into the field but had no idea where he lived. However, after a while we were joined by people we knew. Then two more groups arrived, making about fifteen of us, all on the edge of the field. Then two policemen turned up in a patrol car and they were interested in the circle as well.

So there we were, some in discussion and some striving to gain a vantage point for photographs, when it happened. The farmer arrived on his tractor. He almost skidded to a halt, and leaping off his machine, he told us in terms that left us in no doubt

of his sincerity to get off the edge of his field. Apparently he had thrown some people out of the circle earlier in the day. He was very angry and said he was sure that either students from a nearby school or hippies who were camping in the area had made the circle about four nights before. He gave us his views about crop circles in words that left little to the imagination and with a clarity that ensured everyone heard. So, after saying our goodbyes to everyone and a final glance at the forlorn-looking circle, we all left.

The photographs I took of the circle, which was about 20 metres out from the edge of the field, shows it to be swirled anti-clockwise, partially flattened and approximately 7 metres in diameter.

During the next few days there were conflicting reports of sightings of a UFO over the field and it was said that it had created the circle. A boy was supposed to have been thrown off his bicycle by the UFO. This report was countered by another that said the boy was looking around and ran into the roadside bank. Yet another report stated that a woman driving her car saw coloured lights in the sky over the field just before the circle was discovered. It certainly was an eventful start to the season.

YARNBURY CASTLE
Wiltshire

On 15 May we heard conflicting reports about the location of a dumb-bell-shaped pictogram in a field of oil-seed rape somewhere near Warminster in Wiltshire. This report was too vague to act upon, so we waited for further news. It came after a pilot had spotted a shape in a field close to the very large Iron Age fort of Yarnbury Castle.

We drove to the location and spent an hour or so driving round country roads and tracks trying to find it. We even climbed the ringed defence mounds of the ancient castle, but to no avail. Feeling somewhat frustrated, we went home knowing that the next approach would have to be an aerial reconnaissance.

Fortunately the following day I was invited by the film company Circlevision to take a helicopter flight to try to locate the site. This I accepted and when we were about two miles from Yarnbury I could see a dark shape in a crop of oil-seed rape. Sure enough, when we reached the field we could see a dumb-bell shape depressed into the crop just the other side of a tall hedge alongside the A303. We had been so near the previous day. Filming was carried out by the crew and I also took video and still shots, one of which is shown here.

After several phone enquiries the next day, I contacted the farmer for permission to enter the field but was told that the landowner had said nobody was allowed to go into the field.

Scaling the pattern by the tractor lines, the approximate dimensions were: total length 18 metres; circle on the left 4.3 metres in diameter; circle on the right 3.4 metres in diameter. Both were swirled clockwise. The path was 1.8 metres wide.

We were not having much luck with farmers so far this year: that made two pictograms tantalizingly near but with entry barred to both.

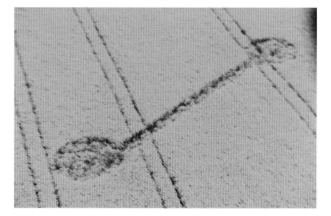

HEASELEY FARM
Arreton, Isle of Wight

On 25 May this single circle was found by Mrs Garratt, of Lake on the Isle of Wight, while taking a walk in the St George's Down area. She phoned me to report it and said the position of this one was close to where there had been other similar ones in previous years but they had been in another field. This one was positioned in the corner of a field containing oil-seed rape. She had examined it as well as she could from the side of the field and said the crop in the circle looked well flattened and undamaged. As far as she could judge, the diameter was about 8 metres.

Mrs Garratt had mentioned her find to Dave Brown, the farmer, who later visited it. I phoned him and he said he could not understand how it came to be there. It appeared to be a perfect circle and the flattened crop forming the floor was not damaged and it was swirled clockwise. To reach the circle the farmer said he had to make a pathway to it from the edge of the field.

Colin and I flew over the field to take photographs and the circle looked very good in the bright sunlight, as did the whole of the pretty island.

PEPPERBOX HILL
near Salisbury, Wiltshire

On 28 May Colin phoned to say that it had been reported on a TV programme that some patterns had been seen in two fields below Pepperbox Hill. We agreed that this occasion called for some aerial photography because we knew from previous years that it was difficult to gain permission from the farmer to enter these fields.

We circled the fields a few times and took photographs of what appeared to be three intriguing patterns, two of them in one field. The pictogram on its own was long and had similarities to the one at Alton Barnes in 1990. Of the other two, one had the outstanding feature of a capital 'A'. The patterning of

them appeared faint and ill-defined because the crop in it seemed to have made considerable recovery to become upright.

Obviously a ground inspection was called for. This we were able to do after some diplomatic discussions with the landowner, who instructed his farmer to allow us into the fields. We made our visit on 31 May after introducing ourselves to the farmer, George Ware. Our first impression of the long pictogram was one of dismay because the crop was almost upright but shorter than that in the rest of the field. We quickly saw that the reason for this was that the part of each stem from the bottom to the

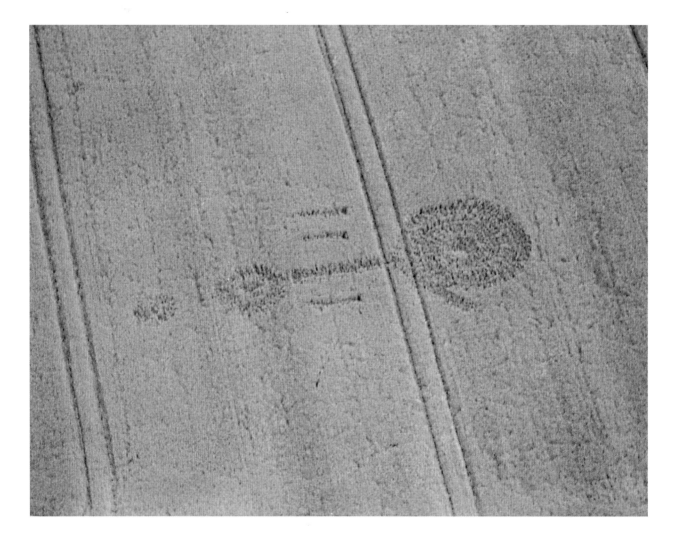

first node was lying flat on the ground. This was the only part of the plants that defined swirl and lay direction. Nothing appeared to be damaged.

We took only a few photographs because the patterns were not photogenic from the ground, but some of the detail was interesting. The wheat crop was immature with undeveloped heads. The total length of the formation was about 75 metres. The 'A' pattern was 16 metres long. The third pattern was 37 metres long. This one had four remote boxes and a remote circle to which no entry marks could be seen so we did not enter them.

KIMBRIDGE
near Droitwich, Worcestershire

Reported by Mrs G. Bell and Tony Coulson on 1 June, this was a ringed circle with an overall diameter of 20 metres. A 9-metre-long corridor projected from one side and ended with a large and small finger to form the now familiar 'key' shape. The circle was positioned a short distance from the Barnwood Link Road.

CHILCOMB DOWN 1
near Winchester, Hampshire

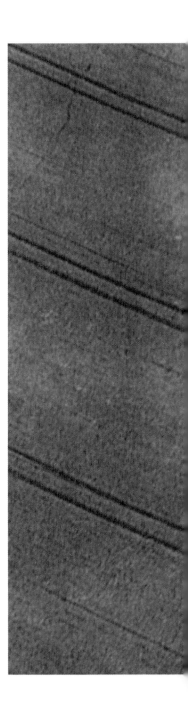

A phone call from Matthew Lawrence early in the day on 7 June had my daughter Jan and me driving with some haste to a point on the A272. This road, leading out of Winchester, has in past years seen thousands of visitors viewing crop pictograms in the fields on either side of it. Here we were again, our excitement undiminished. From the second gate on the right going up the hill, we saw, up on the hill on the east side of the road, some dark shapes of circles and other markings that we could not identify because of the oblique viewing angle. I knew I was not going to be allowed into the field, for it belonged to Farmer Bruce. He is the man who a few years ago was adamant that it was I who was making all the crop circles!

It was going to be a pattern of which I would have to be content with aerial photographs only. It is unfortunate that even though I took these the next day, visitors had walked straight across the field to the pictogram, making the two pathways. The total length was 70 metres.

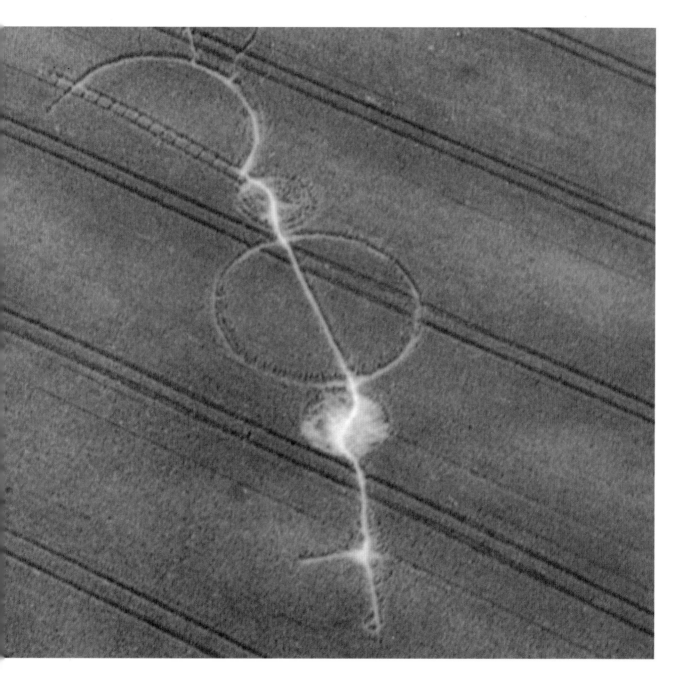

SALTFORD
Avon

This pictogram was one of the first to appear in this area. It has some of the features with which we have now become familiar. However, the pattern also contains a square shape, which is seen at the bottom right of the photograph. The total length was 46 metres.

Unfortunately this pictogram was quickly vandalized and also suffered considerable wind damage.

CIRCLES IN DEVON

A photograph of one of the few circles created in Devon in 1991 was sent to me by Mr A. Trapnell of Devon. It was created in the small village of Tedburn St Mary, which is about seven miles west of Exeter. The photograph shows the swirled floor of one of the two circle formations with a corridor leading into the second circle.

There were two other formations in Devon this year. One was a single circle at Matford, which is about two miles southwest of Exeter. The second was a circle with a half-ring and short corridor at Ashcombe, which is about seven miles south of Exeter.

The farmer who owns the field at Ashcombe said, 'I can offer no satisfactory explanation for what has happened. I am keeping an open mind. If this was done manually, the flattened corn would have taken an awful lot of putting down. It's two hundred yards from the nearest gate and a long way from the road. I'm sure a prankster would not have bothered to walk so far.' He added, 'The circle was created sometime during the night. I have a good view of this field from where I live and the circle is not something I would have missed had it been there any earlier.'

He was even more puzzled when harvesting the field: 'We tried to lift the flattened corn but it was impossible, even by machine. That is something I have never known before.'

Finally he said, 'While I am still keeping an open mind about the circle, I am convinced it was not made by human hand.'

LOCKERIDGE
near Marlborough,
Wiltshire

We flew over this pictogram on 28 June, a few days after it was created. From the air it appeared to be very unusual, with its exceptional length sprawled out across the field and oblique to the tractor-wheel marks.

Observing the formation from the ground a few days later proved to be somewhat disappointing because the circles and rings of the pattern were not well flattened. Although of late we have become reluctantly familiar with non-pristine flattening of some of the pictograms, to me this particular one fell short of total attraction. That is how this subject is; the formations are very personal.

The crop was wheat. The total length was approximately 91 metres. This formation was quickly disfigured by visitors, as most of them were this year.

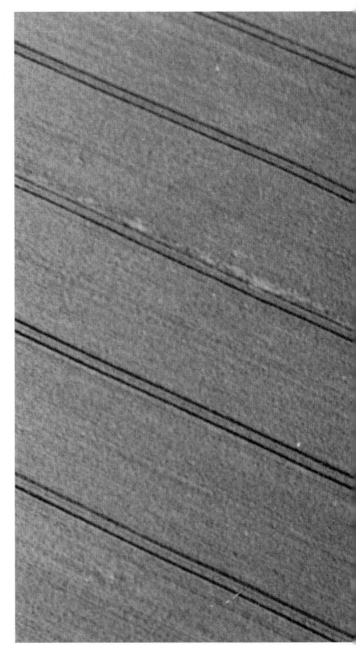

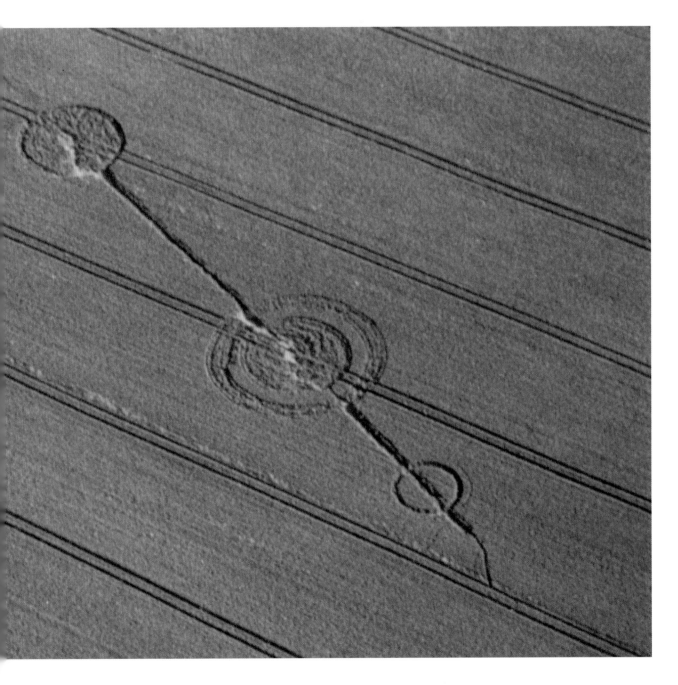

BISHOPS CANNINGS
Wiltshire

This was one of two formations that were created on 28 June in front of two surveillance teams. The sophisticated equipment of both groups failed to detect any activity in the field during the night. The formations were seen in the morning after a blanket of mist had dispersed. The large circle was 16 metres in diameter and swirled clockwise. The small circle was 2.3 metres in diameter and swirled clockwise. The floors were untidy and rough. The surveillance sites can be seen on the hill and to the left of the trees.

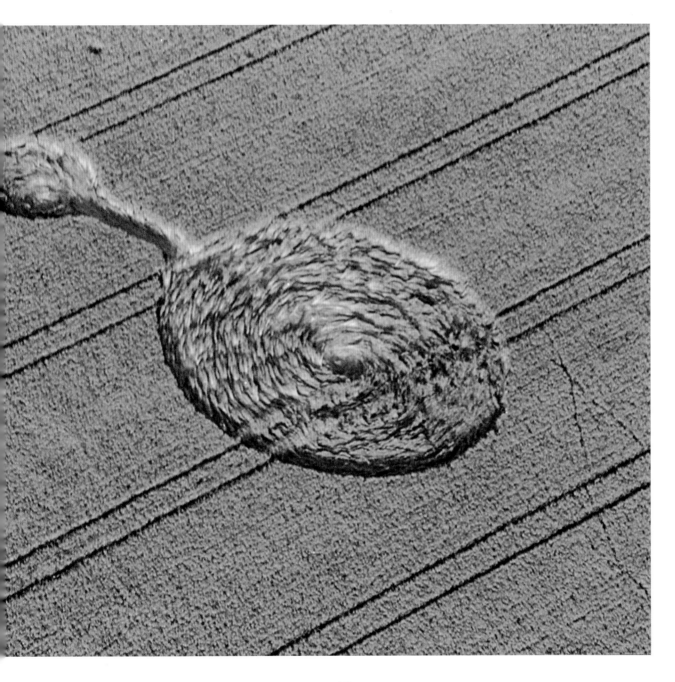

WEST KENNETT 1
Wiltshire

This formation was reported on 29 June. Its length was 46 metres. The larger circle was 19 metres in diameter and the smaller one 9 metres. Both were swirled clockwise.

SEVEN BARROWS
Litchfield, Hampshire

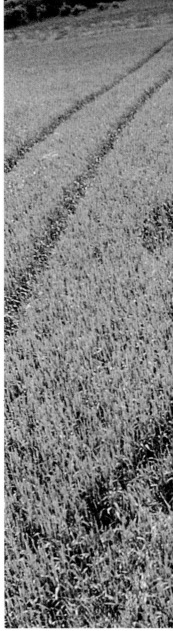

Matthew Lawrence reported this formation on 1 July. The site is close to four of a group of ancient barrows and in the same field. It was at this site that I met Mr James Phillips, the farm manager. He was puzzled by the formation which had appeared in his field and how the affected crop stems were attempting to regain a vertical position from the second node above the root.

The formation was only a short distance from the busy A34 and just a few metres from a public footpath which was also adjacent to a high-tension electricity pylon. The total length of this pictogram was 74 metres.

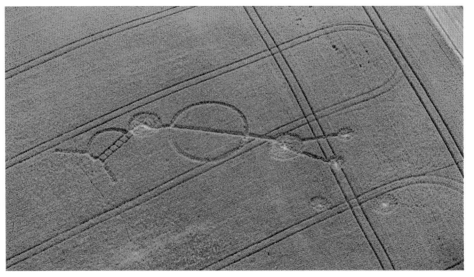

NEWTON ST LOE
Avon

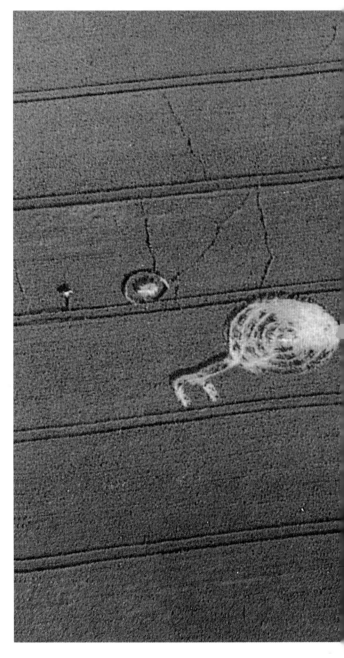

On 30 June Richard Tarr phoned me to report a new pictogram at Newton St Loe. From his description of the pattern it seemed to be so complex that I decided to see it for myself. With the aid of an Ordnance Survey map, we made arrangements to meet at a point close to the site.

The next day I drove off into a part of the country with which I was unfamiliar. I managed to take a wrong turning once and found I was heading in the wrong direction. However, I corrected the mistake after a couple of miles and counted it as a bonus because I was able to look into extra fields.

I met Richard on time and soon we were finding our way via the tractor lines up a steeply sloping field and into the pictogram. There were already four people inspecting the patterns. Two of them were newspaper reporters and when they found out who I was they asked me to give an interview.

I took video and still pictures of the separate elements that made up the long pictogram and also of the swirl and lay patterns. There had not been many visitors and consequently no damage was apparent except for tracks made between the sections. The photograph shows the unique feature of the pattern.

Originally the little single circle on the left had no access track. The circle on the right of the four boxes, which were devoid of entry tracks, was not

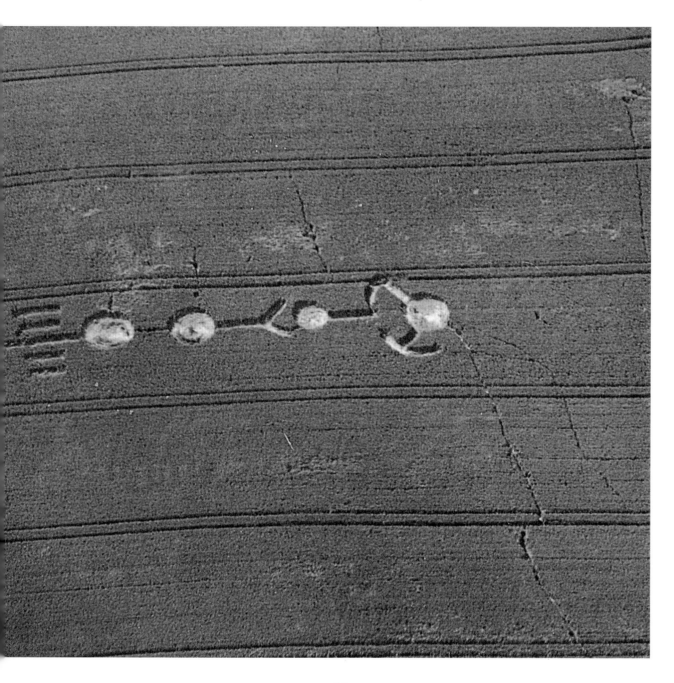

originally joined to the next circle on the right. The bottom arm of the horizontal 'Y' was not originally joined to the circle and the corridor from that circle was not joined to the top arc of the element on the right. Altogether there were eleven separate elements. The total length was 110 metres.

Many more visitors were arriving at the site all the time we were there, and by the time I flew over the pictogram the following day I could see all the extra marks they had made.

MEDINA
Orleans County,
New York, USA

Nathan Elliot of Rochester, New York, sent a very long and detailed account of his visit to a circle in a field of wheat. The circle was discovered by Todd Roberts, son of farmer Lee Roberts, on 5 July 1991. The actual location was in the small town of Shelby, which is close to Medina. The following are extracts from Elliot's report:

We did not hear about the circle in my area until August 1st and it was August 8th before my friend and I drove the forty-five miles to see it.

When we arrived we found it easily because it was close to the road and roped off. The ropes had not done their job because the circle was almost destroyed by all the sightseers who had been visiting it for over a month, it was a huge tourist attraction.

The field had been harvested but we could see that some of the wheat stems in the circle were swirled counter-clockwise; this was most prominent round the edges and most of these were pressed hard into the ground still with the buds on. Towards the centre the pattern began to change to a radial swathe with the stems pointing towards the centre. We lifted some of the stems and it seemed there had

been two layers when it was created, with the under layer being clockwise. The entire pattern was erratic and in some places there were several layers going in different directions.

We measured the diameter and found it to be twenty feet [6 metres]. We took photos, made diagrams and I took some soil samples from the centre.

The farmer had said that when he first saw the circle, half of it was swirled one way and half the other way and it had well-defined edges. It had suffered damage through thousands of visitors being there.

I have spoken to UFO experts about the circle and they think it was made by a UFO. They substantiate this claim by the fact that the soil in which they appear is sterile afterwards. [Not true. P.D.]

CHEESEFOOT HEAD 1
near Winchester, Hampshire

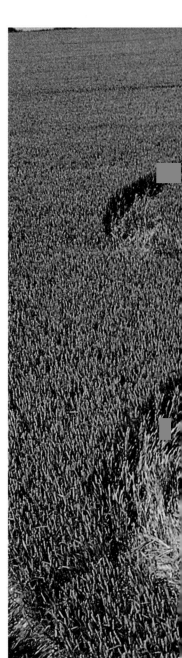

Reported by James Withers on 5 July, this formation was the first to appear in this area in 1991. It was on the other side of the road to the famous Punch Bowl, in the bottom corner of the field, opposite the car park.

The total length was 35 metres, with circle diameters of 7 metres and 9 metres. The ring was 15 metres in diameter. Both circles and the ring were swirled clockwise.

ALTON BARNES
Wiltshire

This pictogram, reported on 7 July by James Harper, was created in the same field and a few metres east of where the large formation of 1990 was positioned. Similar to its predecessor, it was subjected to an onslaught by visitors and so was farmer Tim Carson, who collected their pound coins to view it. What a good idea that was: satisfaction for the farmer and visitors alike. Unfortunately not all fields hosting crop pictograms were in such an ideal location for visitor control as this one.

Perhaps, if the phenomenon continues, we will see a change in the attitude of many farmers towards allowing paying visitors on to their land. However, it must be said that a few farmers are renowned for their co-operation and invite the help of others to find out what is going on in their fields.

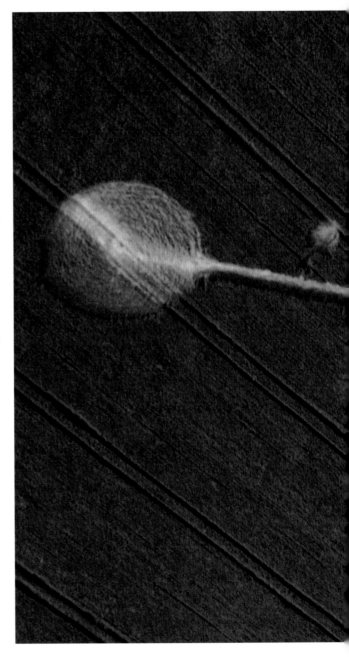

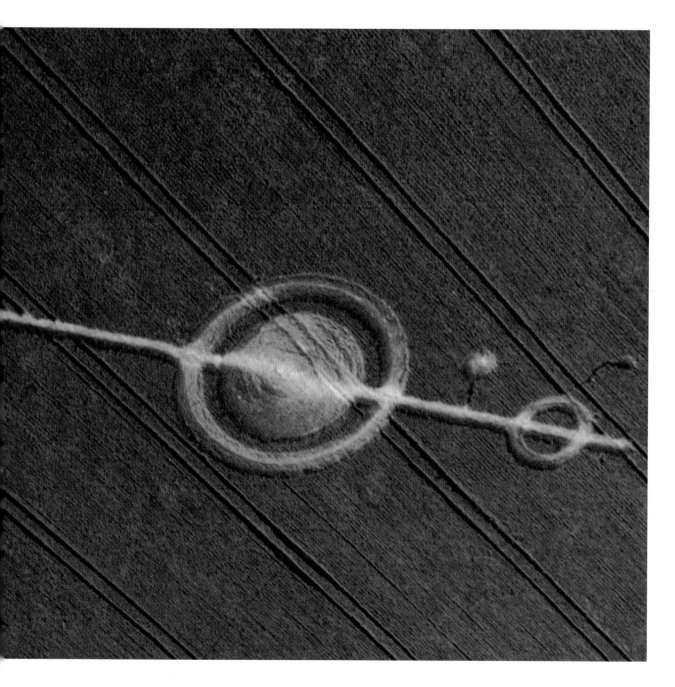

SIXPENNY HANDLEY
Dorset

Reported by Matthew Whitehall and Dr R. Jacobs on 8 July, this pictogram had an overall diameter of 28 metres. The ground photograph was taken from the long corridor, looking into the circle.

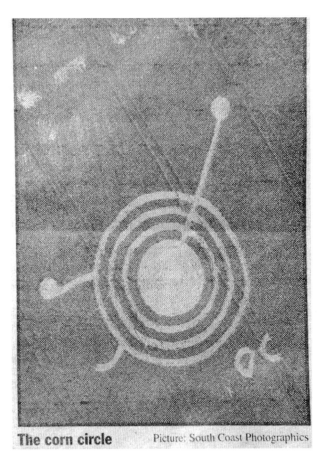

The corn circle   Picture: South Coast Photographics

HACKPEN HILL
Wiltshire

This pictogram was reported on 11 July. Subsequent reports concerned trouble experienced by the farmer while attempting to keep people out of his field. The pattern was approximately 65 metres long. The two large circles were 18 metres in diameter.

LITTLE RUDSEY FARM
Nottinghamshire

Reported by Tony James on 14 July, this was a quintuplet formation. The centre circle was 15 metres in diameter and the satellites were 3 metres in diameter.

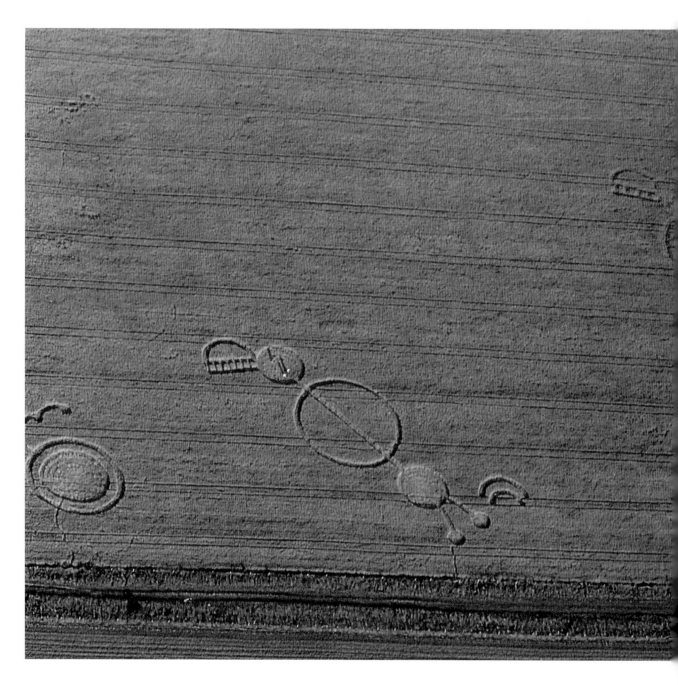

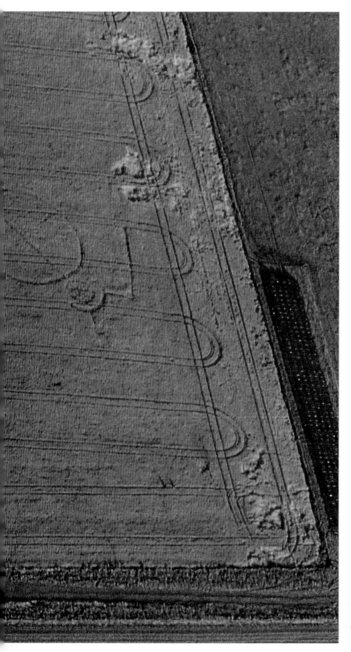

STONEHENGE
Wiltshire

These formations were reported by several people on 12 July. There were two 'laddergrams' and a pictogram in a crop of barley, in one field, just the other side of the A303 and fairly close to the famous stones. One of the laddergrams can be seen to be much fainter than the other. Judging by the way the originally flattened crop had risen and the height of the weeds among it, it must have been created about five weeks before the others.

One of the photographs shows a view looking along the ladder of the later formation directly towards Stonehenge on the horizon.

BROCKENHURST FARM
Nottinghamshire

These two circles in a crop of wheat were reported by Tony James on 14 July. One was 24 metres in diameter and the other 4 metres. The circles were well flattened in a clockwise direction.

FINEDON
Northamptonshire

Gary Rose reported this formation, adjacent to the A510, on 16 July. The floor of the 34-metre-diameter circle had multi-directional lays with a clockwise band round the edge. Most of the stems were undamaged and were bent over just above the ground.

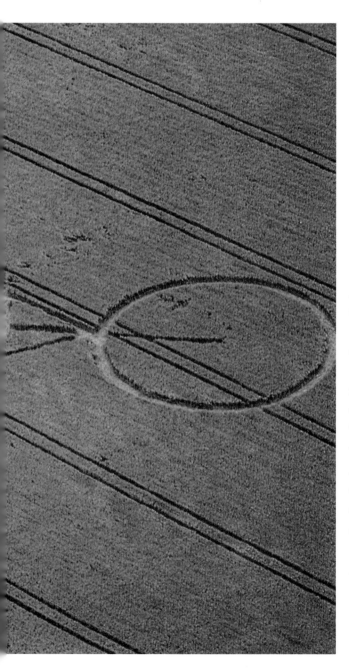

BARBURY CASTLE
near Swindon, Wiltshire

Reports of this formation were received from a number of people on 27 July. Its geometrically sensational character caused shock waves of excitement that lasted a long time. For sheer size and complexity it surpassed anything that had been created so far.

The formation appeared on Overton Farm, between Barbury Castle and the village of Broad Hinton, south of Swindon. When asked about the patterns, Mr White, the farmer, said, 'They're amazing, nothing like this has happened here before. I've no idea how or why they appeared. They certainly weren't there last night.'

There was much controversy about whether the formation was genuine or not. Some said such complex patterning had to be the work of man. Those opposing this argument said it had to be the work of something we do not understand, otherwise many of the other pictograms would be called into question. A great deal of work went into its construction. I calculated the total length of the corridors and ring paths to be 936 metres and the total flattened area is approximately 2340 square metres.

WELLINGBOROUGH
Northamptonshire

This circle, 17.8 metres in diameter, was reported
by Gary Rose on 19 July. The road in the
background is the A45 where it crosses the River
Nene. The clockwise swirl was smooth and orderly,
and the spiral content was about two complete turns.

WOODFORD
Northamptonshire

The diameter of the centre circle was 18 metres.
It was surrounded by six rings, the outermost of
which was 86 metres in diameter. The four inner
rings were very evenly spaced, and the clockwise
swirls were all flat to the ground.

STRANGE EVENT AT LAPWORTH
West Midlands

Because it was such a local sensation, the creation of a 10-metre-diameter crop circle at Lapworth was reported on 19 July by Tony Harding, Kevin Briggs, Sid Moss and Godfrey Nall. Brought to light were two inexplicable incidents that could have been associated with the creation of the circle. Tony wrote to me describing these incidents, which happened during the night the circles were formed.

Incident 1: The morning following the circle's creation, twenty-five of the farmer's sheep were found in a different field from the one they were in the night before. He was told they were found wandering about the field together, frightened and very nervous as though something had scared them.

Incident 2: The farmer was also told that one hundred baby pheasants he owned were missing and that their pens had been flung open with some force.

Tony later reported that the leaves of the large oak tree facing the circle had turned yellowy green very much earlier than the remainder of the tree.

Kevin spoke with the farmer, Richard Lewthwaite, who confirmed that when he discovered the circle there were no access paths to it. The farmer said, 'We've never had anything like this in our part of the world before. It was all crushed in a clockwise direction. The stalks were still green, so it would have taken a good bit of pressure to flatten it. On the night it happened there was hardly any wind, so the weather could not have been to blame.'.

Here are a few further reactions to this circle:

Jasmine Edline, anthropologist, said she had traced an ancient ley line through the field connecting with sixty churches.

Some people preferred the suggestion that the mark was that of an alien spaceship.

The Ministry of Agriculture refused to comment on the possibility of an invasion by beings from another world.

Mother witch Beth Garevitch, who heads the 900-strong First Church of Witchcraft, said, 'It's Mother Nature performing her magic. People feel they must have a logical explanation for things or they do not happen, but they do.'

Weatherman Dean Snowden of the Birmingham Weather Centre said, 'It could be weather-related, a mini whirlwind is one theory. It's just one of those mysteries.'

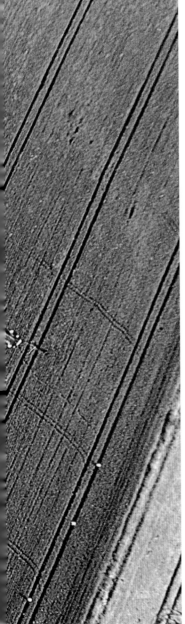

ALTON PRIORS
Wiltshire

Reported by farmer Tim Carson on 19 July, this was a very dramatic pattern 110 metres long on a sloping hillside. I collected for analysis a flaky substance from the top surface of the plants in the largest ring.

CHILCOMB FARM
near Winchester, Hampshire

This formation was reported by Matthew Lawrence on 19 July. It was tucked alongside a hedge and consisted mostly of curled corridors. The aerial photograph shows a small circle on the left side of the pattern. This was not there originally, as can be seen in the ground photograph taken earlier. It was created by a visitor who had a strong desire, it seems, to add his personal graffiti.

WEST LETHBRIDGE 1
Alberta, Canada

These circles on the farm of Fred Watmough were reported by Chad Deetkin. The circle diameters ranged from 2 metres to 9 metres. The woolly appearance is due to the fact that the crop is barley.

The paths made by visitors are obvious when compared with the straight originals.

WARNER
Alberta, Canada

Chad Deetkin reported these circles on Roy Tetzlaf's farm. The anti-clockwise-swirled circles measured 3.2 metres, 4.2 metres and 9 metres in diameter. The diamond-pattern formation was apparently undamaged.

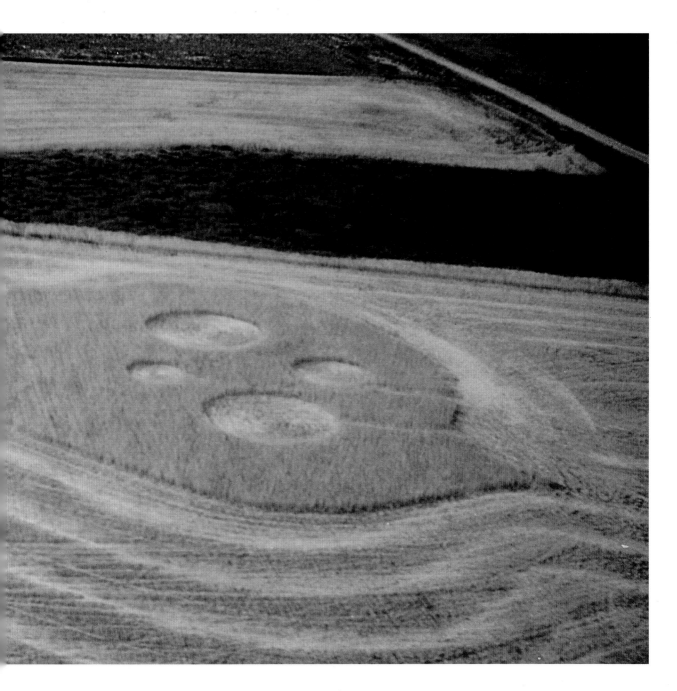

SUTTON 1
Cambridgeshire

This 22-metre-diameter circle with two arms was discovered in a field of wheat about to be harvested. The overall length is 42 metres. The corridor features are unique to this area of England.

UPTON SCUDAMORE
Wiltshire

Reported on 25 July, this was a very long (126 metres) formation centred for its entire length on tractor-wheel tracks. It is accompanied by two small circles and a small pictogram.

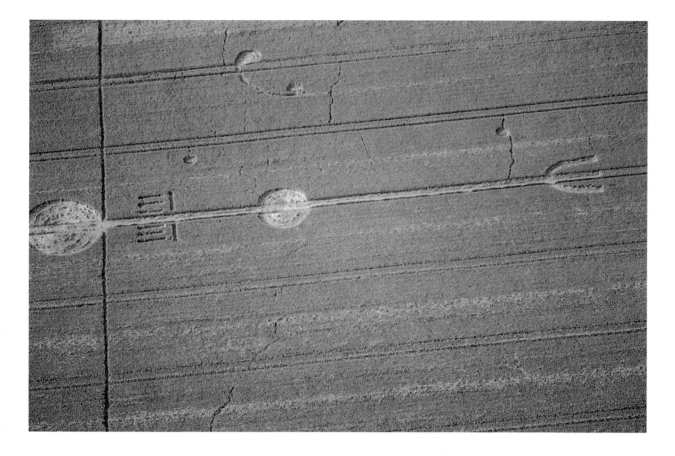

WEST KENNETT 2
Wiltshire

Reported on 27 July was this stark and harshly mechanical-looking pictogram, 94 metres long and seemingly too precise with all its sharp corners and stem-perfect corridor edges. This stark effect is enhanced by the sky reflecting off the crop stems, producing the white 'painted on' look. The pictogram contains a very important feature: there is no access to either of the standing crop-ring centres, where it would seem necessary to be in order to delineate the rings' peripheries.

WEST LETHBRIDGE 2
Alberta, Canada

These circles with corridors (*right*) on Jenny Skinner's farm were reported by Chad Deetkin. They were photographed after harvesting and still displayed the well-swirled clockwise circle floor with the 1-metre-wide pathway flowing into it.

The circles with corridors on Aub Hubbard's farm (*below*), also reported by Chad Deetkin, measured 4 metres in diameter and were swirled anti-clockwise. The 1-metre-wide pathway can be seen to flow *out* of the circle.

SIBSON
near Peterborough,
Cambridgeshire

This formation was discovered in late July. The larger ring was 72 metres in diameter, 4 metres wide and swirled clockwise. The smaller ring was 26 metres in diameter with a 5-metre-diameter centre circle. Both were swirled clockwise.

SUTTON 2
Cambridgeshire

These three separate circles were created in the third week of July. The diameters were 26 metres, 14 metres and 8 metres. All were swirled anti-clockwise. The width of the appendage corridors appears to diminish with circle size.

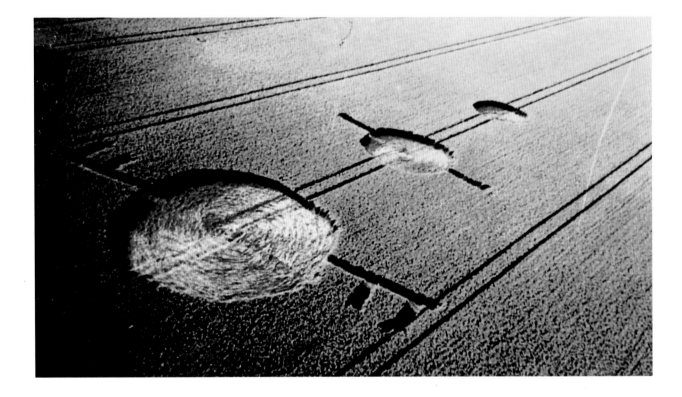

GUYHIRN 1
Cambridgeshire

This odd formation was created in late July. It was 82 metres long and 40 metres wide. The strange half-circle and the wide strip connecting the two circles top left make you wonder what the creator had in mind. The edges of the clockwise swirls were well defined.

AMESBURY
Wiltshire

This curly pictogram was reported on 28 July. The main feature was 46 metres long. The odd single circle, the two crescents and five of the rings were swirled clockwise. The top right ring was swirled anti-clockwise. As can be seen from the ground photograph, the pattern was well defined.

CHARACTERS ON THE GROUND

The exception to circles and geometric patterns in crop formations are letter characters. The first to be recorded were the letters WEARENOTALONE, with the 'N' on the right round the wrong way. This feature, despite its appearance in our book *Crop Circles: The Latest Evidence*, has never been explained.

Mr A. P. Railton of East Yorkshire sent me a photograph that he took of four letters in a field. They were in lower case and were shown as: a p b o. The characters all have a basic loop or circle of approximately 7 metres in diameter except the loop of the 'b', which is the smallest of the four, and its diameter is just over 6 metres. The vertical stroke of the 'a' is 7 metres long and the vertical strokes of the

'p' and 'b' are 14 metres long. The width of the characters is nearly 1.5 metres. The letters were created on the night of 29–30 July 1991. The formation had well-flattened crops and the character edges were well defined. The 'o' was remote from the tractor-wheel tracks and there were no access marks. The crop was wheat.

In a field below Milk Hill in Wiltshire there appeared a strange row of characters with rectangular features. If it was a message of some kind, created in a manner that is not understood, we will probably have to wait a long time before it is deciphered. Worse still, if it is a prediction, it may occur before we are forewarned. If it was intended as a practical joke, then I expect it succeeded in satisfying someone's ego. However it was created, whatever its purpose, there will be those who have tried and are maybe continuing to attempt to decipher it.

The symbols are in a field adjacent to the 'frying pan' pictogram. It is thought that the strip contains two words, meanings or messages as a break seems to be indicated in the centre and at either end. The small rings at each end are thought by some scholars to have significant similarities to ancient writings.

A rather more bizarre example of the appearance of letters on the ground was seen on a hillside in a field of snow near the town of Belsenberg in Germany. The article was sent to me by Dennis Tavener of Sussex, who had received it from Helmut Schäffer in Switzerland. Dennis has very kindly translated it for me from the original German text. The cutting is from the *Hohenloher Zeitung* of 4 March 1991. The letters read NOCH 1 JAHR?, which means either A YEAR TO GO? or YET ANOTHER YEAR?

The dimensions of the inscription in the snow in Künzelsau-Belsenberg were: length of the inscription on the first row of letters 30 metres; total height of the two lines of script 18.6 metres; height of the letters 8 metres; width of the letters 0.7 metres.

The letters were impressed into the snow with extreme accuracy. The photograph was taken some days after it was formed, when the snow was beginning to melt.

PUNCH BOWL
Cheesefoot Head, Hampshire

Reported by Matthew Lawrence on 30 July, this was one of many formations displaying curly features. The outer ring measured 15 metres in diameter, and all the circular elements were swirled clockwise except for the lower ring.

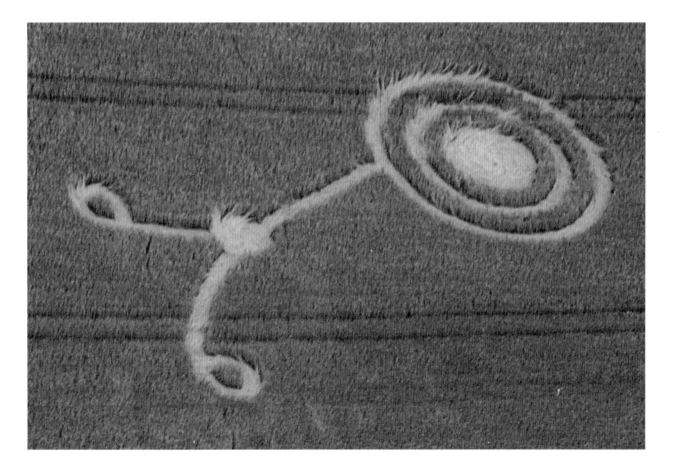

WEST WOOD
Lockeridge, Wiltshire

Reported on 30 July, this was the first of the patterns to acquire the popular 'dolphin' title. It was approximately 110 metres long and because of its size and accessibility it quickly attracted many visitors. They made many extraneous tracks across the field and on one occasion a horse-rider rode to it. The size of the track made on the left of the formation suggests that a pack of hounds went in with the horse.

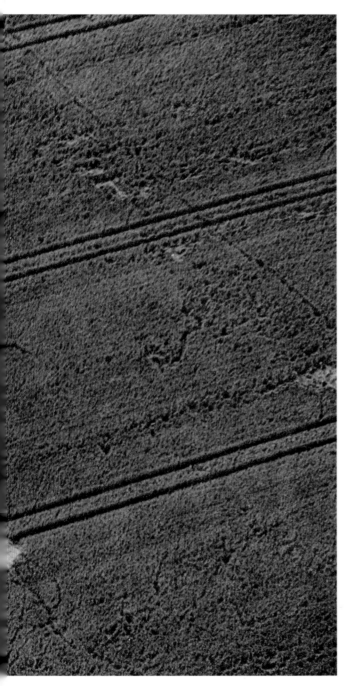

MILK HILL
Wiltshire

The first report of this pattern came on 30 July. Its position in the field below Milk Hill corresponds to where a twinkling light moving over the crops was captured on video last year. The wide ring was 46 metres in diameter. Some have said it looks like two eggs have jumped out of a frying-pan.

FIRS FARM 1
Beckhampton, Wiltshire

This formation was reported on 1 August. It is one of the three 'dolphin' formations which became prolific in this area. It was 42 metres long and the rings were 15 metres in diameter. The lower ring was swirled clockwise and the upper one anti-clockwise.

BECKHAMPTON
Wiltshire

Reported on 1 August, this was another of the 'dolphin' patterns that seemed to favour this area. As is usual in a barley crop, the formation has a slightly untidy appearance. It was 40 metres long and had a tightly wound, clockwise centre swirl. Both rings were swirled clockwise.

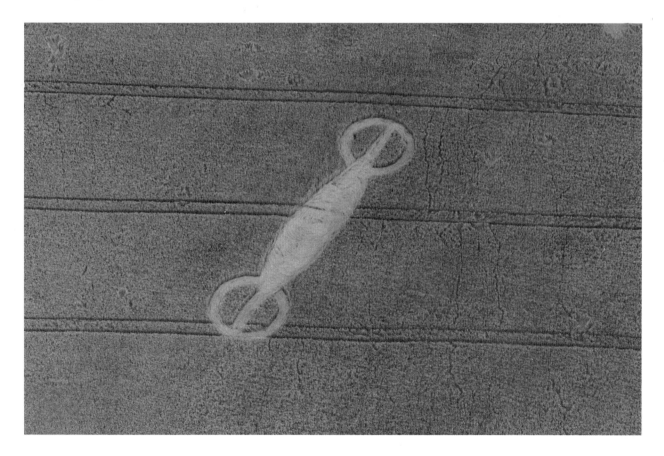

Firs Farm 2
Beckhampton, Wiltshire

Colin Andrews reported on 1 August this long 'dolphin' pictogram with two small circles. The pattern was 78 metres in length. The rings were 1.7 metres wide, and the two fin-like features were 9 metres long and 2.5 metres wide. The lower ring measured 14 metres in diameter and the upper ring 18 metres.

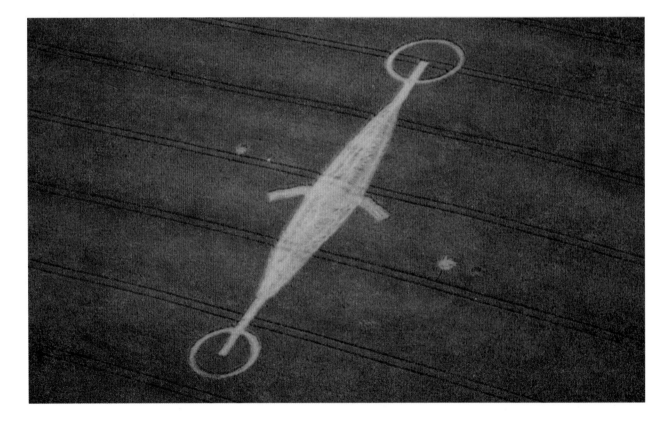

AVEBURY AVENUE
Wiltshire

On 2 August Jürgen Kronig reported this 'dolphin' pattern. It was created at the southern end of the avenue and on the east side of the road. It was 30 metres long and the rings were 13 metres in diameter.

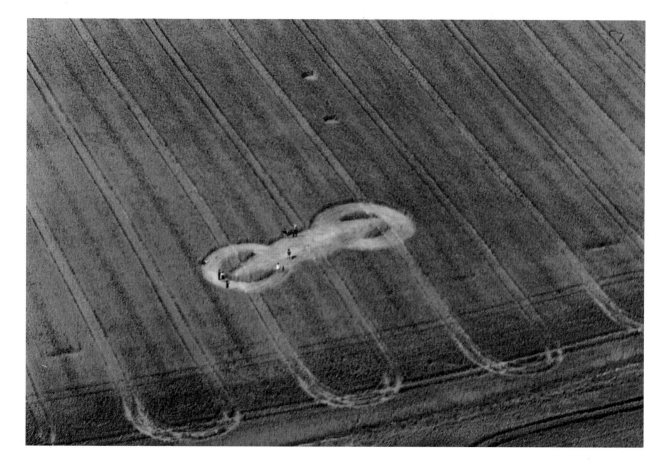

BENTWORTH
near Alton, Hampshire

Reported on 2 August by Kit Neilson, this was a 'traditional' ringed circle in an idyllic location on a sloping hillside surrounded by trees. Both the 21-metre-diameter circle and the ring were swirled clockwise. We had to call in at the local pub to enquire where it was and the locals, who knew all about it, willingly gave us directions.

TWYFORD DOWN
Hampshire

We spotted this formation when returning from a photographic sortie on 2 August. It was in a crop of barley and although it showed up well from the air when the sun was at a low angle, it was almost invisible from ground level, as the photograph shows. The 42-metre-long main formation and the two adjacent ones were all ill-defined. This led me to estimate that it had been created about seven weeks before my visit. I took the ground photographs about an hour after I had taken the aerial shot.

GUYHIRN 2
Cambridgeshire

This irregular formation was found in early August. The circle was 52 metres in diameter and was not a true circle, as can be seen. The unattractive pattern is reminiscent of some small deep-sea creature. The dark streaks visible in the field are the remains of ancient dried-up water channels.

SPALDWICK
Cambridgeshire

Found in early August, this 30-metre-diameter circle had four quadrant rings of 72 metres in diameter at the end of radial corridors. The circle and the arcs were all swirled anti-clockwise.

SEARBY
Humberside

News of this circle was sent to me on 3 August by Mr A. Wetherell of Stallingborough, Humberside. He also sent a newspaper cutting about it and a photograph.

At the beginning of August farm foreman Andrew Spilman was combine-harvesting a field at Searby Top Farm when he spotted it. He said, 'I looked out of the side window and there it was. I pulled up straight away and left the area around it.' He added, 'I'm a bit dubious as to what has caused it, but you never really know.'

Mr Strange, the farmer, said, 'It is such a symmetrical circle with a perfect pattern of concentric rings. It is certainly not man-made. There are no tracks into the circle from the outside.' He continued, 'The Ministry of Agriculture suggest it may be a pattern that has been made by a wind vortex. But whatever caused it, it really is an amazing thing.'

Searby is midway between Scunthorpe and Grimsby. The circle was in barley, and was 14 metres in diameter and swirled anti-clockwise. Circles created in barley always have a woolly appearance, owing to the loosely hanging crop heads.

KEYSTON
Cambridgeshire

Found in the first week of August, this dumb-bell formation had a large circle of 24 metres in diameter and the smaller one was 11 metres in diameter. The satellite circle was 7 metres in diameter. All were swirled clockwise.

WEYHILL
Hampshire

Reports of this formation came from the farmer on 5 August. A strange feature is the way the flattened corridor on the right of the circle extends across the green kale strip. The kale was completely unaffected. The large circle was 16 metres in diameter, with an open, anti-clockwise swirl. The small circle was swirled similarly.

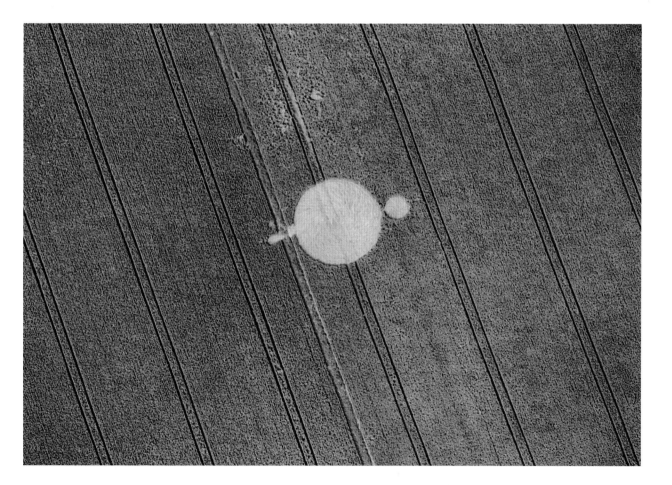

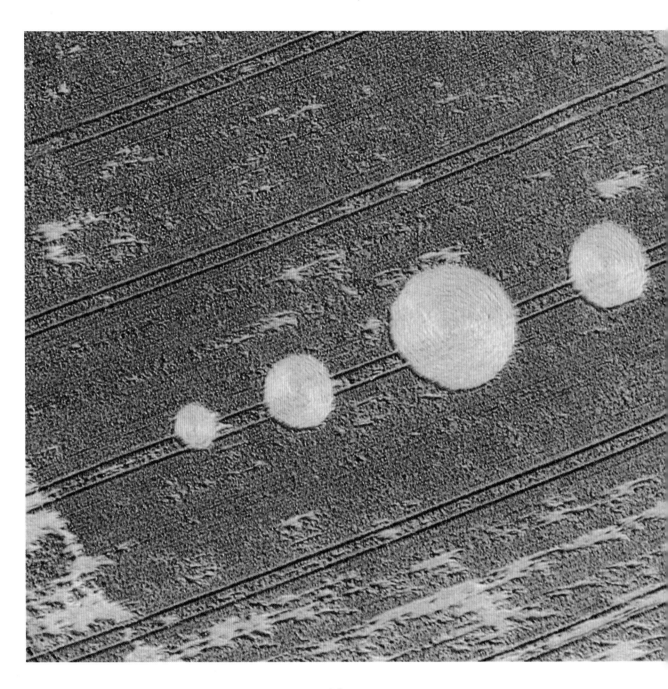

MONXTON
Hampshire

This formation was reported on 5 August. All the circles are swirled anti-clockwise and their diameters are 5 metres, 8.2 metres, 8.7 metres and 14 metres. As can be seen, the field had suffered considerable wind damage. The other photograph shows Paul Norman, the Australian UFO researcher, discussing the circles with me. Colin took the photograph.

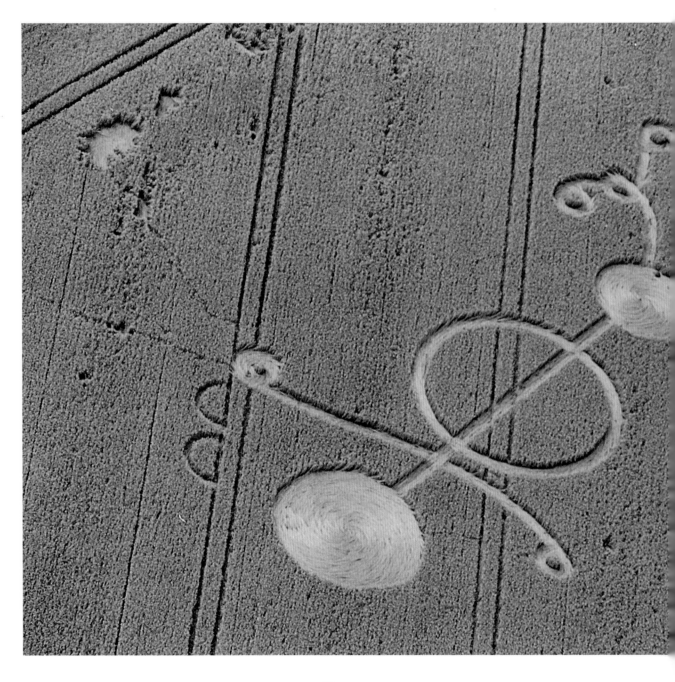

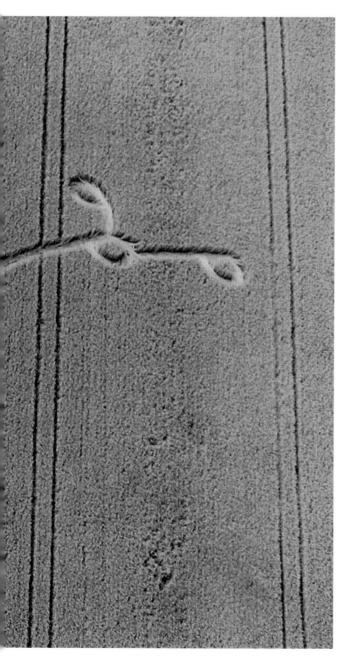

KITELANDS
near Micheldever Station, Hampshire

We first sighted this curly pictogram alongside the A303 soon after take-off on 9 August. It was 63 metres long and 42 metres wide. The two circles and the large ring were swirled clockwise, and the small rings were swirled in the direction the corridors led into them.

CHILCOMB DOWN 2
near Winchester,
Hampshire

Peter Thaesler reported on 6 August this 16-metre-diameter ringed-star formation. It was positioned in a steeply sloping field and well below the level of the adjacent A272 road. The two attendant crescents are again prominent – as, unfortunately, are the disfiguring tracks left by visitors who did not stick to the tractor-wheel lines.

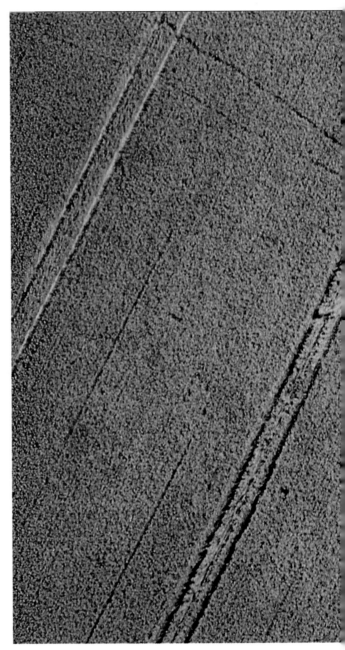

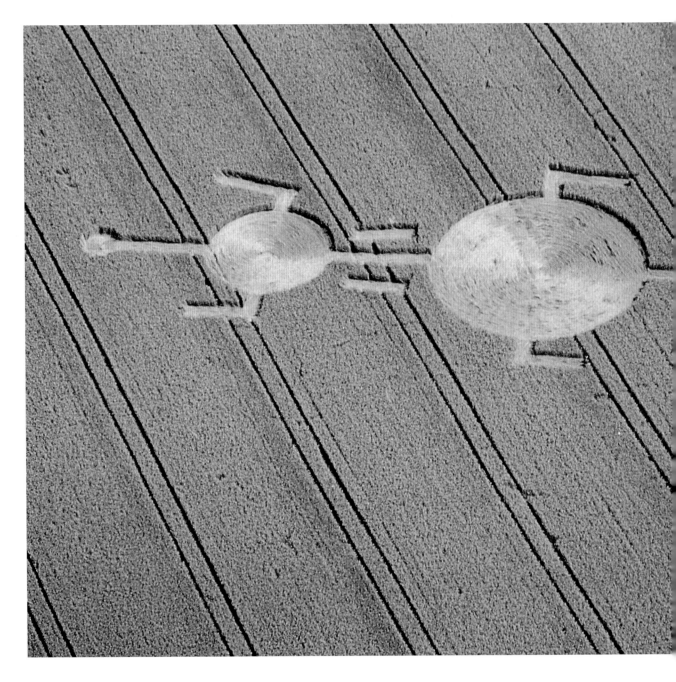

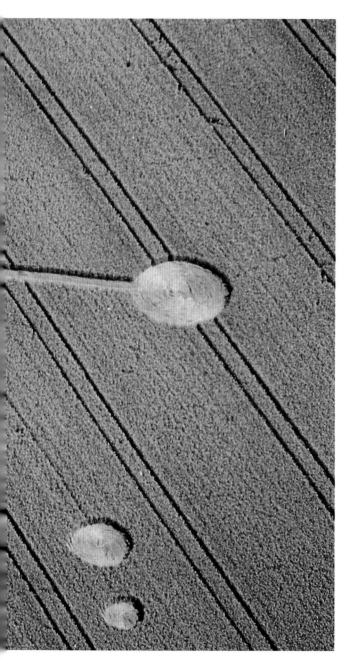

CLATFORD
near Marlborough, Wiltshire

Reported on 15 August, this 78-metre-long, four-legged shape was the formation where two German brothers videoed a strange small, glowing ball of light floating over the top of the crop. The farmers who own this field emphatically discouraged visitors, as many who tried to enter will verify.

WILTON
Wiltshire

This 180-metre-long pictogram, reported on 15 August, was a beautiful sight as we flew over it in the setting sun. It was located along the top of a long, ridged hill and accompanied by a mini-pictogram signature.

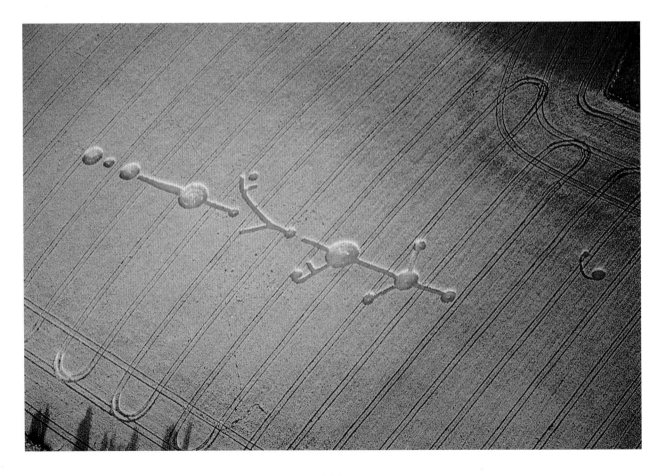

THE MANDELBROT SET

On 13 August 1991 pilot Steven Cherry-Downes flew over a wheat field at Ickleton in Cambridgeshire. What he saw in that field started one of the greatest crop-circle controversies since serious research of this phenomenon began.

The flattened shape he was gazing upon was significant to him in that he had never seen anything like it before. Its true significance only became apparent two days later when an aerial photograph of it appeared in the *Cambridge Evening News*. Then things really became exciting because it was realized, among scientists, mathematicians and computer programmers especially, that they were confronted with a replication of a form known as the Mandelbrot Set.

The term 'Mandelbrot Set' describes a mathematical pattern that was discovered by a French mathematician, Benoît Mandelbrot, in 1979. It has yet to find a mathematical use. For the following explanation of this complicated pattern I am indebted to Mr John Sayer of Corpusty, Norfolk:

There is an undeniable progression in the complexity of the crop formations. For example, the Barbury Castle pattern reached the highest level so far but still maintained a definite geometrical basis.

The Ickleton Mandelbrot Set represents to date, a logical conclusion to the crop formations' development. Previous formations have been of an artistic or representational nature. They not only look like something – they are something.

The Mandelbrot 'goes one better', a quantum leap away from school-book geometry. It takes us into the realms of chaos theory, fractals, computer technology and infinity. The Ickleton formation does not look vaguely like something – it is the Mandelbrot Set and if it means anything, it means all or some of what the Mandelbrot means.

Considering the possibility that a non-human intelligence is at work here, if it is a 'mundane' life-form inhabiting the same universe, we can safely assume that it is more technologically advanced than we are. It would also be logical to assume that the circle-makers have an equal, if not greater, understanding of mathematics and science. Our own attempts to communicate with other possible life-forms are designed by mathematicians and scientists. If we imagine this process in reverse, we can assume that anyone else trying to communicate in this universe would also use mathematics, technology and science.

In the search for 'meanings' of the crop formations, we could conclude that the circle-makers have been trying out various symbols from various cultures, perhaps even as an overture, to prepare us for a more definite 'sign'.

The Mandelbrot Set is not derived from any particular culture; its mathematical base is universal. Being unambiguous, it would be an ideal symbol for one species to use to communicate with another.

In conclusion, what we have here in crop formations is either Earth-bound human intelligence which possesses the most guarded secret technology in the world, and has been able to operate without detection for at least thirteen years, or non-human intelligence which is deliberately and methodically trying to open up a channel of communication with the inhabitants of this earth.

I am also very grateful to Mr George Sassoon of Warminster for sending me the following informative explanation of the Mandelbrot Set:

The Mandelbrot Plot [sic] was only discovered by Mandelbrot, who works for IBM, a few years ago. It is a product of pure mathematics and of chaos theory. If the corn figure at Ickleton matches it to any accuracy and the figure can be shown not to be the work of hoaxers, you have the ultimate proof that there is some unknown intelligence behind the crop circles.

He continues:

The Mandelbrot Set is perhaps the strangest thing yet to be found in pure mathematics – a hideous, obscene, menacing figure, resembling some foul, poisonous parasitical insect. Its bulbous body with its two fat buttocks is surrounded by what could be small round feet and at its front is a perfectly circular head, joined to the body by a narrow neck, with a thin, projecting, bloodsucking proboscis. The entire ghastly creature is surrounded by hairs, bristles or cilia of some kind.

This figure is not the work of some delirious, drug-crazed artist but the result of a simple mathematical procedure which can easily be implemented on a home computer.

It was discovered in the course of research into chaos theory, which includes the study of what happens when a mathematical procedure is repeated endlessly on a number. Take for example the following procedure. [I include this for the many mathematically interested readers. Apologies to those of you who are not. P.D.]

1. Think of a number.
2. Square it, and add to the number.
3. Square that and add to the original number.
4. . . . and so on.

What happens? In most cases, as for all positive numbers, the result just gets bigger and bigger, finally disappearing into infinity. But for numbers between 0 and -2, it does not; the result hops around but stays within a small range.

For less than -2, it disappears in the direction of plus infinity. Zero and −2 always come back to the same number:

0 squared + 0 = 0.
0 squared + 0 = 0.
−2 squared = +4 which +(−2) = +2.
+ 2 squared = +4 which +(−2) = +2.

Suppose we draw a dot on the graph for numbers which do not diverge to infinity, and leave the rest blank, we get the 'Mandelbrot Set for real numbers', a rather boring line from −2 to zero.

To get something exciting, like the Mandelbrot Set, we must extend this technique to complex numbers. Complex numbers are not really complicated, they are simply numbers that come in two parts, the real and the imaginary. In algebraic terms, real numbers may be written as A or X, while complex numbers would be (A,B) or (X,Y). They can be plotted as points on graph paper, the vertical direction usually representing the imaginary part, the horizontal direction the real part.

The rules of arithmetic for complex numbers are very simple – you just treat the imaginary part as if it was a multiple of the square root of –1 and then do the arithmetic in the usual way. Thus:

$$(A,B) + (C,D) = (A+B, C+D)$$
$$(A,B) - (C,D) = (A-B, C-D)$$
$$(A,B) \times (C,D) = (AC-BD, BC+AD)$$

Division is rather more complicated – you have to do what is called 'rationalising the denominator' to get rid of the imaginary part on the bottom line:

$$\frac{(A,B)}{(C,D)} = \frac{(A,B) \times (C,-D)}{(C,D) \times (C,-D)} = \frac{(AC+BD, BC-AD)}{S}$$

where $S = C^2 + D^2$, a pure real number, by which AC, BD, and AD can be divided individually.

Obviously it is possible to raise these number to powers and do all the other things that can be done with pure 'real' numbers. There are even complex prime numbers, known as Gaussian primes, which have all sorts of interesting properties.

If we use the same algorithm, start with a number (A,B), keep squaring and adding the original (A,B), and plot points where the result does not disappear to infinity after, say, 100 iterations, we end up with the Mandelbrot Set, the hideous bug.

This of course involves hours of work using a home computer, but there is a new one using 286 or 386 language that does it in a few minutes.

It is for this reason, the amount of computing required, that the Mandelbrot Set was not discovered until the 1980s. What is incredible about it is that such a simple procedure can generate such a complicated figure. You can enlarge it, explore the tendrils and filaments that go out from its edges and if you use enough iterations, you find everywhere smaller and smaller versions of the original figure.

In case you require a little more help to think 'Mandelbrot', this third explanation is given by Mr Matthew C. Gregory:

It is a mathematical shape generated by a simple equation $(Z \rightarrow Z^2 + c)$ that is unique in having infinite detail. Any successive magnification yields yet further fine detail. It is a 'fractal', being self similar at any level of magnification.

Chaos theory is a recent scientific revelation of great importance. Many systems can be scientifically analysed and their futures predicted. Others, from quite simple logic, fall into 'chaotic behaviour' and are unpredictable since an infinite degree of accuracy of measurement is required to predict a future state.

Imagine a number line:

```
+···+···+···+···+···+···········to infinity
0   1   2   3   4
```

These are actual counting numbers – the entire line can be thought of as a set (collection) of numbers. In mathematics this is called 'N'. Now of course there are negative numbers:

```
to infinity······+···+···+···+···+···+·········to infinity
              -3 -2 -1  0 +1 +2 +3
```

This set is called 'R' (real numbers) and contains 'N'.

There is another set of numbers called 'C' (complex numbers), which is the above set 'R' plus imaginary numbers called 'i', which cannot actually be written down. Graphically, it can be seen that the space above and below the line has been ignored. This is where the imaginary numbers go. Since they have a value and cannot go left or right of '0' on the horizontal line, they must go either above or below the line:

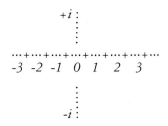

```
+i :
   :
   :
···+···+···+···+···+···+···+···
-3 -2 -1  0   1   2   3
   :
   :
-i :
```

The addition of these two vertical axes has produced a graph and the space between them and the horizontal axes is called the 'Argand Plane'; it is a two-dimensional flat plane. A 'complex number' is a number that represents a point on this plane. For example, the complex number 3 + 2i gives a point on the plane where 3 is along the real axis and 2i is up the imaginary axis.

```
2 : . . . . . . . × This point represents
1 :                the complex number 3 + 2i
···+···+···+···+···+···
-1  0   1   2   3
```

The Mandelbrot Set is a collection of points on this plane. Each point on the plane is tested to evaluate its membership of the Mandelbrot Set.

The equation $Z \rightarrow Z^2 + c$ is applied to the point being tested over and over again. Every time the equation is applied the point moves to a new position on the plane. If, under many applications of the equation, the point shoots off to infinity, it is not a member of the Mandelbrot Set. If it settles down to a point on the plane then it is a member.

The Mandelbrot Set is thus neatly centred on zero on the Argand Plane. It is a 'fractal' and has the following properties:

1. At any magnification it looks similar.

2. The pattern boundaries are infinitely long, infinitely twisty and infinitely detailed.

3. Increasing magnification reveals more and more detail.

There are infinitely more fractals but only one Mandelbrot.

It is seen in the photograph that the Ickleton formation is practically a faultless replication of a

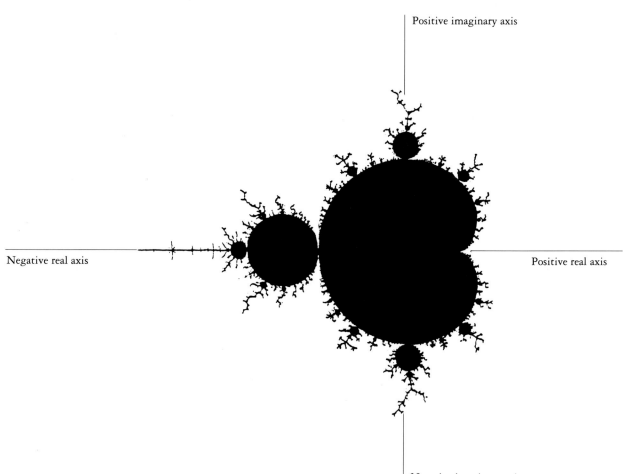

Positive imaginary axis

Negative real axis

Positive real axis

Negative imaginary axis

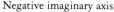

true Mandelbrot Set. Now we know what is demanded of even a powerful computer to create this pattern on paper, how was it created in a crop field? The formation measured approximately 56 metres at its widest part, and there was about 280 square metres of flattened crop.

Now that this particular computer technology has risen to its present level, maybe the creation of this infinite chaos pattern in the crop field was intended as a parallelism. We have had 'real' and 'imaginary' axes explained in accepted terms. So it is but a short step to apply the same logic to our 'material' and 'spiritual' axes, the Argand Plane representing the membrane between these two realms.

SILBURY HILL
Wiltshire

Colin saw this formation on 16 August while flying over the area. It was odd-shaped, 58 metres long and placed in the corner of the field. It was located about 400 metres south of the famous hill. All four circles were swirled clockwise. The circle diameters measured 2 metres, 5 metres, 9 metres and 24 metres.

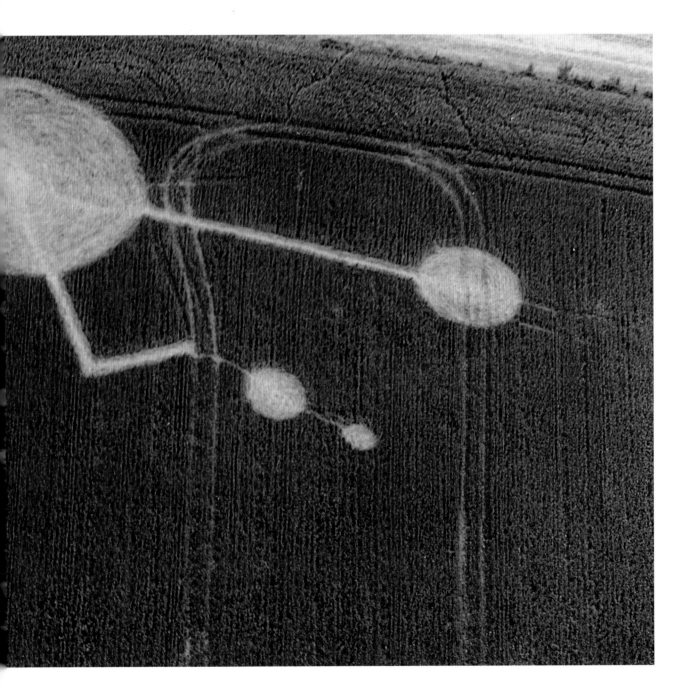

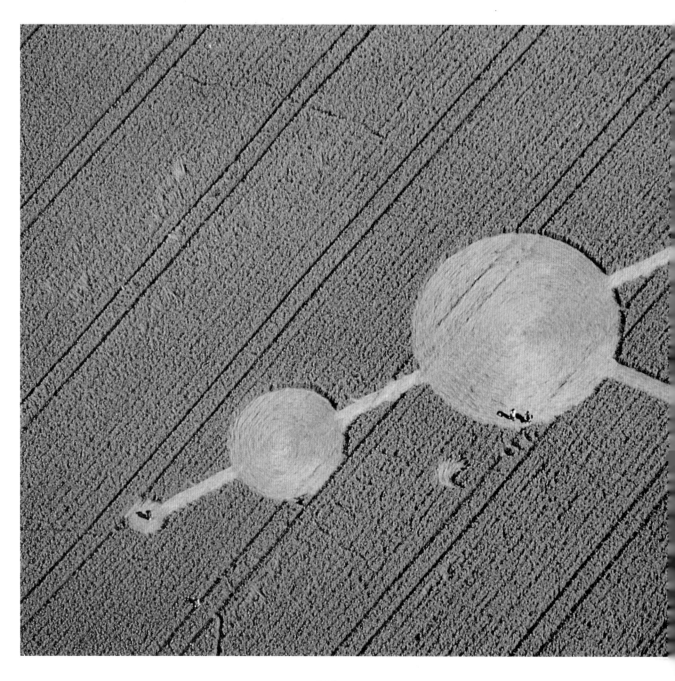

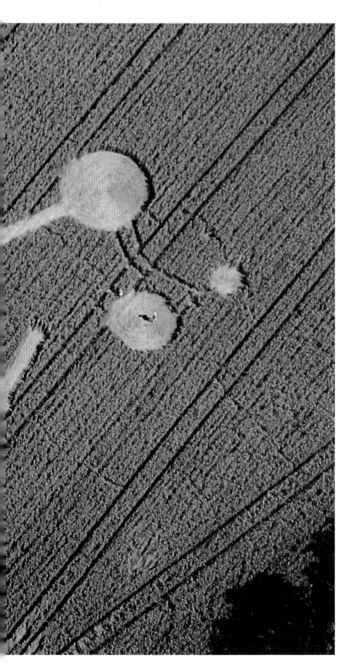

CLENCH COMMON
near Marlborough, Wiltshire

We saw this pictogram on 16 August while on a photographic sortie. Created close to the corner of a field, it rapidly became one of the crop-circle-spotters' favourites, especially for picnic parties.

CHEESEFOOT HEAD 2
near Winchester, Hampshire

Many reports were received about this pattern on 16 August. It was in the same field as the first pictogram at this location and a similar pattern to the first star shape created lower down the hill, except this had a second ring and an adjacent ring-ended path. The overall diameter was 26 metres.

W YE
near Ashford, Kent

This formation was reported by Dr and Mrs King on 10 August. We see here a ground view of the three circles and corridor that made up this pictogram, which had a total length of 42 metres.

LONGWOOD ESTATE
Cheesefoot Head, Hampshire

Reported on 17 August, this was a cheeky-looking creature-type formation, dubbed the 'snail'. It was 27 metres long and the length of the tail was 8 metres. All the circles were swirled clockwise.

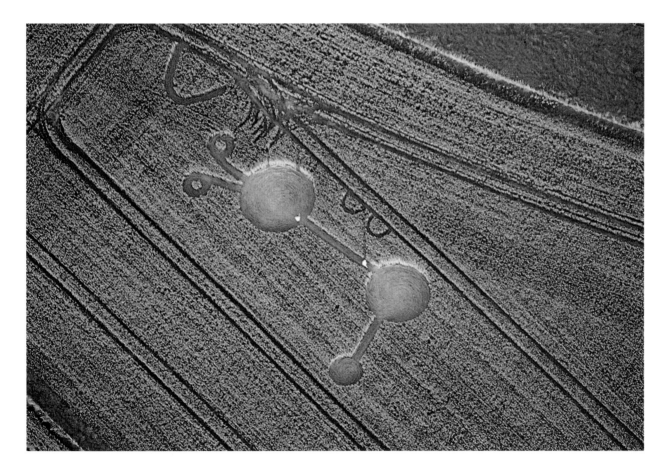

FROXFIELD 'BRAIN'
Wiltshire

Reported on 18 August, this controversial
formation, the so-called 'brain', is different
from anything we have seen before. It was only in the
field for five days but that was long enough for us to
secure ground and aerial photographs. Studying the
pattern, it appears that some of it is remote from
access and I did not enter these areas because it
would spoil the aerial shots I intended to take the
following day. The area of the pattern was about 800
square metres.

FROXFIELD 'DOLPHIN'
Wiltshire

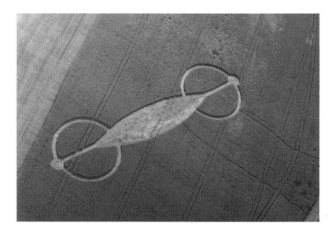

This 'dolphin' pattern was reported by Jürgen Kronig on 18 August. It was 85 metres long and was preserved from harvesting for one day. Fortunately I was able to take this photograph a few hours before harvesting was completed. The rings were 28 metres in diameter and both were swirled anti-clockwise.

FROXFIELD 'BUG'
Wiltshire

We found this formation from the air on 18 August. It was a friendly-looking bug-like character with its four little legs. Could it be that these four features were the start of two intended rings? The body was 25 metres long.

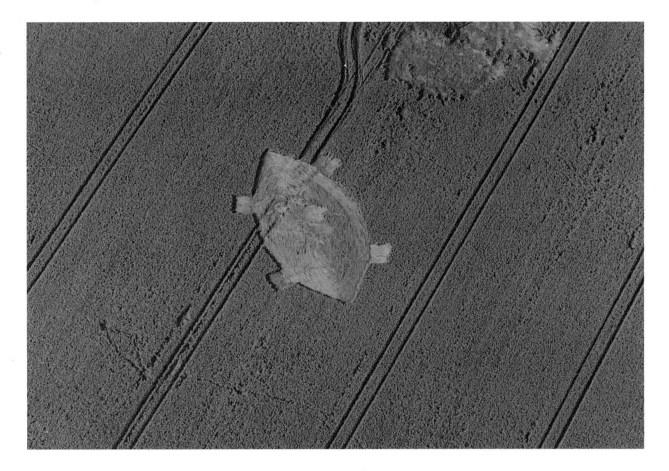

A Study of Hoaxing

The dictionary defines a hoax as follows: a humorous or malicious deception, cheat, trick, fraud, prank, bluff, etc.

One of the events of 1991 was the claim by two elderly men, Doug Bower and Dave Chorley, that they had created all of the crop circles in southern England for the past thirteen years. They claimed they had made all of the circles from Warminster in the west to Eastbourne in the east and as far north as Wantage. They also claim that they created the pictogram in Kent that the newspaper *Today* invited me to inspect on 5 September 1991. I accepted this offer and met the reporter, Graham Brough, who escorted me to the field.

After casually walking through the formation without carrying out the more thorough checks we normally do on these occasions, I said it appeared to be well formed and was quite a work of art and at that stage I said I thought it was genuine. Then I decided to take some photographs because the sun was dropping towards the horizon and it was already being obscured by thick haze. After taking the photos I decided to carry out some checks for electromagnetic noises in the formation by using the tape recorder's earth probes. These are pushed into the ground and connected to the input socket of the tape recorder, which in crop circles considered to be genuine would normally gain some response. It was then, when I was unable to pick up any distinctive noises at all, that I became perturbed about the situation. By this time the reporter had long gone and there seemed little point in prolonging my visit, so I left the site.

On Sunday 8 September, Bower and Chorley were brought to my house by Graham Brough to tell me that they had hoaxed all the circles in central southern England. The reporter said he believed their story because he had been with them for a week. Later, when I was recalling what had been said, I realized that two men could make a good job of making a pattern in a field given two or three days in daylight and the co-operation of the landowner. I have not been offered any photographs or video that would prove they hoaxed this formation or any other.

A detailed article covering both episodes appeared the next day in *Today*. It included photographs suggesting the two men had hoaxed the Kent circles but there was no topographical reference in them. They could have been taken anywhere. The article was concluded with the words, '*Today* has paid no money. © MBF Services.'

A considerable amount of investigation uncovered nothing but confusion as to what role MBF had played in the affair. The letters apparently stand for Maiden Beach Farm, which is located near Crewkerne in Somerset. On 4 November 1991 I gave a lecture on crop circles to the Foreign Press Association at their headquarters in London. Graham Brough was there and I had occasion to ask him about MBF and how they were involved with what I considered to be a fraudulent scam. In front of the audience he said, 'It was a joke. The words were added as a joke.' One now wonders how much of the whole episode was a joke and how much professional journalistic standards have been violated by it.

To this day I have not been shown any photograph or video that records the two men making at least one circle; not a shred of evidence that would substantiate any of their claims.

Another group, the Wessex Sceptics, have joined the growing band of hoaxers and duped several people this year. They seem to take great pleasure in this – and these are people who are employed by our universities. Colin and I met them on a TV show. They were disruptive and provocative and this stance has no place in serious research.

Investigations so far have brought to light a well-orchestrated misinformation and debunking campaign that suggests it was initiated last year by 'official departments' and at ministerial level. There are at least two other countries involved in this network of intrigue. The two self-professed hoaxers seem to be but pawns in a plan to discredit many of us associated with the phenomenon. When *Today* broke the news about the men's alleged hoax, a press statement was issued worldwide stating that I had said all the crop circles were hoaxed. This is untrue. I have never said that all the crop circles are hoaxed.

This incident is seen by many people to be the cover-up that it really is. People ask why 'official departments' insult our intelligence in this way. Seemingly the phenomenon is subject to the same procedure as that applied to UFOs. I feel the reason for the 'official' concern is the enormous surge of interest in crop circles throughout the world, including among professional and scientific people and people in high places. It may be of some concern to them that the phenomenon can carry very significant spiritual connotations by opening up people's awareness and unifying them beyond belief. It could be seen as some kind of threat.

The whole episode has been a real test for the subject and I am touched by the overwhelming support I have received from people all over the world. Claims of hoaxing have occurred in the past and I am sure this will not be the last.

SURVEILLANCE

Watching and waiting is the basis of surveillance and recent years have seen more and more participation by people who want to do just that.

Setting up surveillance to capture the creation of a crop circle can be easy or difficult, depending on the operation's size, sophistication and location. A large operation with hi-tech equipment requires responsible and to some extent qualified personnel. Without the back-up of reliable people, the whole surveillance is in jeopardy. The location can present problems because a high vantage point is needed to gain maximum vision and detection. Of course, under these circumstances it is difficult to remain unseen and covert, and if the site is easily accessible visitors will be attracted to it both day and night. This can create many problems, particularly with security for the equipment, and interferes with careful vigilance.

However, once you have chosen a fairly secure site with reasonable access and permission from the landowner, you can start thinking about what equipment and personnel you require. A portable generator with a good supply of fuel is vital. Other essentials are: rosters with personnel of varying abilities on each shift; intruder alarms over the area to be surveyed; external equipment which can be used in all weathers; car-parking adjacent to the site;

a good supply of food and water; and toilet facilities.

The basic requirements for a covert operation are inaudibility and invisibility, so as to see yet remain unseen. Professional advice, perhaps from the army, would be useful here.

Before setting up a surveillance operation we should spend a little time considering the subject we are dealing with and what we are trying to achieve. Perhaps the very act of setting up surveillance guarantees nothing significant will be seen, heard or recorded there. We should not be so arrogant as to think we have the initiative in the matter of crop circles. I am sure we do not. For instance, look at the two highly sophisticated surveillance operations which took place in 1991: Project Blue Hill and Project Chameleon. They were sited on the top of Morgan's Hill, near Bishops Cannings in Wiltshire, for the same period. Despite highly sensitive night cameras, radar and intruder alarms, two pictograms were created one night in the field below the equipment and all it took was a patch of mist to prevent detection. It can be deduced that whatever the intelligence behind the pictograms' creation, the limitations of the equipment must have been known by it and avoided.

Let us examine the proposition that crop circles are created either by human agency or by an intelligence from another dimension. Take the first possibility. If you were thinking about making a crop circle in a particular field, would you not put the site under surveillance for a while – 'stake it out' before acting? As for the second possibility, it would be utter arrogance to assume that we are superior to such an intelligence and able to catch it out.

With the initiative heavily on the side of the creators, it is little wonder that when we mount a surveillance circles are often created elsewhere. Probably the only solution for the UK is to have a synchronous satellite overhead carrying out continuous surveillance and then maybe circles would appear only on cloudy nights – unless someone knows differently.

There are some less scientific but nevertheless equal benefits associated with watching together in a group through the night. Many of us have participated in some wonderful conversations, especially when conditions are enhanced by a dome of glittering stars, or even meteor displays from time to time and inexplicable lights and sounds. All this creates unity and an air of expectancy.

AFFECTED CROPS AT CULLOMPTON
Devon

In August 1990, farmer Dennis Emmett of Pond Farm, Cullompton, in Devon, discovered three marks in one of his wheat crops. One of the first news items about it was a lengthy feature, broadcast by the BBC's Plymouth studio in the *Spotlight* programme. The marks were described as being two circles and one triangle, all with well-flattened floors.

Doug Cooper of Honiton, Devon, was alerted about the formations and to satisfy his curiosity promptly drove to the farm, situated a few miles to the north of his home. He had previously arranged to meet Mr Emmett at the site and when they walked out into the field it became very obvious to Doug that something really bizarre had happened. He was confronted with three depressed shapes as had been described: two circles and a triangle.

One of the first things Doug noticed was that there was no access into any of the shapes. They were remote from the tractor-wheel lines. The next thing was the way the circles were flattened: the crop was laid out radially from the centre and not swirled. The triangle contained a gentle swirl.

Doug took some photographs and recorded that the circles were 5 metres in diameter. The triangle had sides of approximately 4 metres in length. In the photograph (page 130, *top*), only the nearest circle can be seen because the ground falls away where the furthest circle is located, left centre of the picture.

On 3 November 1990 Doug phoned me to report that Mr Emmett had asked him to go to his farm again because he had discovered something quite unbelievable. Doug, again with his curiosity aroused, drove to the farm and, accompanied by the farmer, went to the same field as before. This time they were confronted with patches of withering winter wheat in the exact places where the circles and triangle had been in the previous summer. Not only were there withered crops but they were withering in the shapes of the circles and triangle. The crop in the field was at the two-leaf stage and the affected plants were in very poor condition being about two-thirds the height of the healthy ones. They were yellowy green and all leaning over in one direction. They looked very different from the rest of the field. Doug took some pictures of the patches, making sure he was standing close to the spot where he took photographs in the summer.

Back at his house that same day Doug had occasion to check his watch at 6.55 p.m. and discovered that it had stopped at 3.20 p.m. He remembered that this was the time he had reached the triangle in the field. He flicked his watch and it started again and has not stopped since. How many times have we heard similar reports concerning the behaviour of watches in a crop-circle environment?

That same evening Doug phoned me and I was

utterly amazed as he described what he had seen in the field. I asked him if he could return there and collect some plant samples for analysis. The following day he very kindly collected samples of the affected crop from two of the patches, one from the triangle and one from one of the circles. In fact, he extracted whole plants complete with soil around the roots. He also collected unaffected plants and soil growing 100 metres away from the affected ones. All the samples were packed into plastic bags and posted to me.

I sent both the affected and unaffected samples to Mrs D. Di Pinto of Delawarr Laboratories in Oxford, who very generously undertook to carry out limited analysis. Her report is as follows:

I have made an analysis radionically of these samples and enclose a report of my findings. I can only relate to elements and trace elements and I hope something meaningful may be derived from this. My impression is that a fierce, intense and quick heat rather like an exhaust pipe with its gases and acids has denatured the soil and destroyed natural elements.

Mrs Di Pinto supplied the following analysis:

Unaffected sample		Affected Sample	
Vitality	70%	Vitality	50%
Nitrates	70%	Nitrates	30%
Phosphates	60%	Phosphates	30%
Sulphur	60%	Sulphur	30%

No elements registered as being in excess.	Elements in excess. Cobalt. Carbon. Molybdenum. Titanium. Plutonium. Zinc.

As can be seen from this report, it is difficult to draw any conclusions. Why there are differences in the state of the plants is not understood.

I decided to contact another laboratory as I thought it would be interesting to have a second analysis done, maybe by a different method. I contacted Albury Laboratory in Surrey, whom I have dealt with before, but their company had been restructured and I was unable to reach the person I had known previously. After that I contacted Harwell Laboratory in Oxfordshire and spoke to a Mr Terence Carter, who was most helpful. Although none of their departments was able to assist in the required type of test, Mr Carter suggested other government departments in the country where I could at least enquire.

I was given department names in Maidstone, Slough and Harpenden. By the latter I was given information that made me realize the futility of trying to draw any conclusions from analysis results. Mr John Jenkins explained the difficulty: 'If you take two samples of plants, one healthy and the other unhealthy, and they have been growing adjacent to each other, you can discover the chemicals contained in the healthy plant which are absent from the unhealthy plant. What you do not know is why they are absent from the unhealthy plant when they have both undergone identical treatment.'

I continue to hope that one day we will be offered the assistance of an analytical laboratory in the UK, instead of relying on the generosity of researchers in other countries, where we can send a steady supply of crop and soil samples, in order that we may progress in our understanding of the crop-circle phenomenon.

PHOTO ENIGMA AT WYTHALL
Worcestershire

Sheila Watkins of Wythall reported the unexplained presence of a strange object in a photograph. She reported that in late August 1991 Ann Jones of Astwood Bank, Worcestershire, was taken to see a crop circle at Wythall that had formed at the end of July. Unfortunately the field had been harvested but the circle and the well-trodden path leading to it were still evident. She decided to return to the site the following day and take her camera as she had never visited a circle before and wanted a photograph before the field was ploughed.

It was late evening when Ann took two photographs a few seconds apart. When the film was processed she saw there was an object on the first photograph but not on the second. Ann said she was surprised at the result because she did not see anything like the object when she was in the field. The object also appears on the negative, which

produces a clearer image of its position in the circle, whereas it is not clear in the photograph whether the object is near or distant. The negative shows it to be about 1.5 metres above the ground at the perimeter of the circle. A photographic technician explained that the mark could not be an emulsion drip and also that, if it was a flash reflection, there would be a diffused effect and not a clear shape.

When the object is magnified a blue, six-pointed star can be seen at the centre.

This report adds to the many anomalous effects seen on photographs associated with crop circles. Among these have been patches of blue or red haze over circles and small white and black shapes. The phenomenon of crop circles has many peripheral mysteries.

GRASDORF
near Hildesheim, Germany

This is one of the formations that had a dramatic effect on the public when it was first shown by the media. The general opinion was, and probably still is, that it was a hoax. I was unable to visit the site owing to other commitments, but however it was created it required a great deal of energy. I have calculated that the curved and straight corridors or pathways are a total of 108 metres in length and the total area of the circular features is 502 square metres. This makes the total flattened area approximately 600 square metres. Its size and precision attracted many people and, as happened at Alton Barnes, the farmer, Herr Werner Harenberg, charged admission, doubling the fee overnight as the crowds grew.

If the shapes are intended to be meaningful symbols then their creator is the only one who has the benefit of that knowledge.

ATMOSPHERIC VORTICES

The whirlwind theory continues to be the basis of some theorists' idea of how the crop circles are created. This theory was among the first to be considered the most likely candidate. In the early 1980s Dr Terence Meaden, who is a meteorologist, stated that all crop circles were created by whirlwinds. The theory maintained popularity for a while, especially with those who were not fully aware of all the details that constituted a crop circle.

Since those early years Dr Meaden's original whirlwind theory has undergone many modifications and each new version, with its vortex basis, was published as being the one that was now creating the circles. The problem was the crop-circle patterns were evolving and becoming a little more complex. It was becoming increasingly difficult to make his current vortex theory fit the facts – hence the modification. The basic whirlwind component of the theory was changed to a 'stationary or standing whirlwind'. This required special topographical features for it to form and then carry out the circle-making function on crops on the leeward side of a hill. This is stated in Meaden's *Journal of Meteorology*, Volume 10, No. 97, page 78.

In 1990 and 1991 we were seeing very complex patterns in the crop fields and we were now told that the capabilities of an atmospheric vortex had grown to such an extent that it was responsible for the new pattern features in the crops, such as corridors, squares, rectangles and triangles. It was further published that to accomplish these shapes the renamed 'plasma vortex' broke up close to the ground and, depending on how it broke up, it was able to precisely place the various crop-pictogram features that formed the pattern.

Published in *Circles Research 1*, the proceedings of the conference at Oxford 1990, Meaden's plasma vortex theory is substantiated by the Japanese scientist Yoshi-Hiko Ohtsuki of the Department of Physics at Waseda University, in Japan. The article describes how he carried out a laboratory experiment, showing that by discharging charged particles on to a steel plate covered with aluminium powder he was able to create a hole in the powder. It will be interesting to see the transposition of this experiment to a field of wheat.

So here we have a condensed history of the struggle to keep abreast of the evolving crop-circle phenomenon by continuous modification of the atmospheric vortex. The atmospheric 'whirlwind vortex', the atmospheric 'standing whirlwind' vortex and the atmospheric 'plasma vortex' – each in its turn has been claimed in print to be the positive creator of crop circles and pictograms.

Because of the considerable doubt and disbelief concerning the validity of Meaden's vortex theories, many have thought it high time the advice of an official meteorological body should be sought. It was exactly this that prompted freelance writer Ruth Rees to contact the headquarters of the Meteorological Office in Bracknell, Berkshire. Her question to them was simply: 'As the official body of meteorology will you please inform me if it is possible for any kind of atmospheric vortex to create crop circles and pictograms?'

Her question was passed to the Reading, Berkshire, office of *Weather*, a monthly magazine for all those interested in meteorology, published by the Royal Meteorological Society. I am indebted to Ruth for permitting me to publish the following material from the reply she received, written by an RMS Board Member:

I presume that the 'vortex' shapes referred to by Ruth Rees are similar to the one presented in the August 1991 edition of Physics World. *This shows a line of four large and two small circular patterns, connected by a straight line (where the crop has also, presumably, been flattened). Also connected to this line are shapes resembling the letters 'E' and 'C', together with a set of short parallel lines straddling the main straight line. Visible nearby are other very small clusters of circles.*

Almost certainly such patterns cannot be the result of atmospheric vortices, due to the sharp angles that appear to be present in the shapes and also because of the elaborate, organised nature of the patterns. Real vortices possess rather indistinct edges – where the velocity gradients gradually decay outwards from the centre – and they are basically

circular in cross-section. Flattening of the crop in a straight line could result from a travelling vortex, but then we would expect the line width to be similar to that of the circle diameter.

A vortex is, in its most general sense, any fluid flow possessing vorticity. There are many types and sizes of meteorological vortices, ranging from the large (such as depressions) to the small (tornadoes) and even smaller.

Vorticity is a three-dimensional property of the field of motion of a fluid. For many scales of motion the component of vorticity that meteorologists are chiefly interested in is that which occurs in the horizontal plane (i.e. rotation about the vertical axis) rather than the vertical component of vorticity.

A practical example of such a horizontally-rotating vortex is the 'bath plug' vortex. In a horizontal plane through the vortex, the pattern may be represented by a pattern of closed streamlines (at least close to the centre of the vortex); streamlines are lines parallel to the flow at any given instant. In addition to this horizontal motion there is also present a vertical component to the velocity (the water draining down the plug hole) together with a horizontal meandering of the whole vortex (with its base remaining rooted above the plug hole).

Atmospheric vortices, such as a tornado, also contain a vertical component of motion (witness the lifting of debris) while the vortex itself usually travels horizontally in response to larger scale features of the atmosphere – i.e. the background wind field. Two commonly seen vortex structures that can be seen on weather maps are the depression and the anticyclone; these also possess some vertical motion and they rotate in opposite directions.

Many small-scale vortices, such as dust devils and water spouts, do not have a preferred direction of rotation; they are often found to rotate cyclonically and anticyclonically.

Terence Meaden's article in Weather *(January 1989) illustrated several circular patterns that all exhibited remarkable symmetry; the fact that such symmetry is so unusual in a complex fluid such as the atmosphere (especially near the ground where frictional effects come into play) has naturally led to a sceptical response on the subject from the meteorological community.*

This, then, is the official view of the Royal Meteorological Society. The foregoing statements have finally put an end to the claims of Dr Terence Meaden by stating in no uncertain terms that atmospheric vortices are not responsible for creating crop circles or pictograms.

Let us have no more publication of unsubstantiated claims.

INCIDENT AT HIGHLAND
Kansas, USA

Shortly after midnight on 28 September 1991 I returned home to find on my answerphone an urgent request to call a friend, Diane, who lives in the USA. I phoned her back right away and was amazed at what I was being told. The gist of the conversation was that she had been told of significant markings that had been created during the night of 26–27 September in a field which was about 150 miles from where she lives. She intended to visit this site the next day and asked me what information should be sought while there. I suggested that after contacting the farmer a number of photos of the marks should be taken from different views, and sketches should be made of the apparently bizarre shapes that had been described. Also, she should take plastic gloves with which both affected and unaffected soil and crop samples should be taken and put into plastic bags.

Two days later I received another call from Diane and listened to an amazing account of a series of events that Diane and her friend Julie had experienced during their visit to the site. Later Julie wrote to me and Diane sent me an audio tape, both detailing their visit to the site. Code-names are used instead of real names for reasons which will become apparent. Nearly all the text is direct quotation, for I considered that authenticity would be maintained if I presented as much of it as I could in this manner.

The whole incident commenced during the morning of 27 September.

Julie wrote as follows:

In the morning I received a phone call from my friend, Laura, in Highland, Kansas, telling me that she had seen fluorescent blue/green lights, twenty or more, in a field outside of her home. She said she couldn't tell what time it was, as she had no clock upstairs where she was but she was awakened in the middle of the night to find all of the windows open and she was freezing to death. She also said she hadn't left the windows open before she retired but she did try to get up and close them. When she attempted to move, she found herself paralyzed from the waist down. She did manage to roll enough to see out of the window at the head of her bed and that's when she saw the lights.

The next morning there was all the activity at the end of her block, it was roped off. There were a number of men in suits and ties, which is pretty obvious in small town America, driving navy blue and unmarked sedans. There were, like, white vehicles and there were three red hazardous waste removal tankers marked UN 1205 and animal disposal trucks all over the little town. These men blocked off the fields for about two square miles and went from door to door asking if anyone had seen anything unusual. Laura claimed that only her water bill had arrived early and gave no inkling of what she had witnessed.

Later Laura went up to the bar because the man who runs the bar is also the farmer whose property this was on. She asked him what had happened and he had said, 'You and I both know what happened last night,' and left it at that. He then said he would bring her something that evening.

Now what he brought her was a sketch of the formation that he had found in his field that morning. When he brought it to her that Friday night she tried to ask him some questions and he was very shook, he would not talk about it. He said, 'I can't talk to you about this but I wanted to give this to you for some reason,' then left.

Laura is an over-the-road truck driver and is familiar with the codes and serial numbers which semis are supposed to display by law, so that the Department of Transportation may identify what the truck is hauling. She phoned in the numbers (UN 1205) she had seen on the waste trucks but found no listing for that number.

At this point Diane takes up the story:

We got up there about 10 a.m. Highland is a very small town, a farming community of about 500 people, very quiet on a Sunday, no farmers out in the field or anything. My friend Julie went with me, she'd been with me to the circle in Odessa last year.

We met with Laura and her friend who lives down the street from her. I talked with her friend who runs a small radio station where there is local news. There was no news coverage of whatever happened there as far as the government cars coming in, the tankers, which is very strange in itself that this would not be covered.

At Laura's house she showed us the farmer's diagram of what he saw. By the way, I asked her what type of person he is. Just sounds like he is your classic farmer who would not have much interest in crop circles or anything like this, no reason to have made up something like this. What he wrote down are letters and numbers depending on whether you are looking at it from north or south.

The width of each of the characters is anywhere from seven to ten feet and the length of the characters is anywhere from ten to thirty feet. What he had, if you are looking at it from the south, is an E and what appears to be a 9 and a 7 and at the end is either a T or a cross or a plus sign. If you are looking at that from the north side it would be other symbols, E, G, etc.

So after this we proceeded to try and find out where it was on this diagram. He had drawn his house in relation to the formation.

Now, his property must have been about five square miles and it was crops of corn and sorghum and beans and something around most of it. We did not want to go up to the house and enter that way. We just thought it would not be a wise thing to do, so we drove around to the other side, which, as the crow flies, is about three miles from the house, and I have photo evidence of all of this.

There was an open gateway. We went in there and it was helpful because Laura has grown up in this community and she knows when things don't look right, you know, are misplaced or anything unusual.

Now what I didn't realize was, when we drove into this other side of the field my watch had stopped. From that point I looked over to where the house stood and where I thought the formation might have been. I saw, you know the

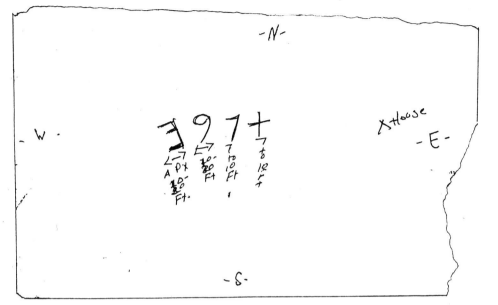

Photocopy of the original scrap of paper on which the farmer drew some of the symbols as he looked at them in his field in Highland, Kansas

way the sun hits the field, that there were lines or something unusual in the field and I said 'That is where it is,' but it was as though they hadn't heard me. They searched around up on that hill for twenty minutes.

In that area where we came in, one thing was strange. There was a crop of corn, part of it had been harvested and the other part was as if something had cut off the tops of the corn. The stems were just cut at the top, maybe about a foot of them. Laura could not figure out why they would do something like that or what could have done it.

There was a pathway wide enough for a vehicle cut through this crop and lots of heavy vehicle wide tire tracks, the earth was really packed down.

We figured out where this formation was on the opposite side of the valley. We walked through two or three fields that had barbed wire fences, the creek, and finally got up to the field. Everything had been only a barbed wire fence but when we got to the field right next to the formation, at that fence there is now a hot wire, a new line. Laura had said farmers do not use hot wire, it's a small town and there's no reason, it's very costly. So that in itself was rather strange.

Anyway, we found our way under the hot wire and we were truly amazed at what we saw. My view is that the farmer only saw, for whatever reason, about one third of this formation and I estimate it was about a quarter of a mile long, yes, it was huge and about thirty to forty feet wide. There was this whole strip of where you could see the demarkation edge of where the normal crop had been harvested, you know how the corn stands up straight and it is cut six or seven inches from the ground and then you drop down to where this formation had been done. It was completely flat.

My watch started again when we reached the formation. I noticed it had lagged an hour.

What it appeared they had done, they had taken those crops, they had shredded them, they had attempted to plough this up, there were parts that were ploughed.

Now the very strange thing, and this is really exciting and is the way we saw this from the opposite hillside, is that it was very, very white and the surrounding crops were that medium shade of brown that they are when you harvest them.

All the husks lying on the ground were very, very white as if they had been treated with a chemical all along the formation.

The second thing we noticed that was very strange was the shredded crop that was laid down over the formation. [An attempt to diffuse the shapes? P.D.]

There were partial husks and whole husks of corn cobs with husks still partially on them but there was no corn in there, no corn whatsoever, those cobs were completely stripped of corn.

We walked along the formation and I could see that they had a great deal of difficulty in cutting and ploughing this because the stems were just bent, the plough couldn't cut them.

It was all in formations and swirls, the crop was flattened to the ground and you know, it was really hard because they had torn it up so badly, but we could see where they cut these crops and let them sit. I could see the demarkation of the diagrams.

Who cut the crops is the big question. I suppose it could have been the farmer. He came in and didn't like what he saw and did it. Then we have the other element of the

Heavy truck tyre marks
entering field

Symbols looking east   Symbols looking west

government being in there, these huge tankers being in there and all the activity and it being roped off which is not a normal thing at all. My gut feeling is that they did it.

The symbols the farmer drew on the diagram were in the middle of the formation. I walked up in both directions from there and from what I could gather, there had been formations on either side extending out in each direction. It was hard to recognize all the different shapes because it had been torn up so badly, but you could see there would be a partial shape where they didn't hit it with a plough or whatever they went at it with. There would be the beginning of a swirl and a bent stock, you know, and if I had not been in Odessa last year, the day after when they cut it down, I wouldn't have known what to look for. They had the same problem there, they could not cut that crop, it was so flat to the ground and some of the swirls were still there in either direction, a quarter of a mile I would say, by my estimation. Anyway, there was something definitely written out all along that length.

It's overwhelming, I talked to Julie today, it kinda feels like a dream and the difficult thing was we brought in dowsing rods, we brought in the pendulum, we brought in the tape recorder, we wanted to work with the energy. But it was too windy for the rods and we both had the distinct impression that we were led there to do our job and leave very quickly. It was like there was no time to stand there and figure out what had been written or discern what energies were there, just get the samples, get the pictures and leave quickly.

We sensed a very ominous feeling of secrecy there and the intense amount of energy that had been put into covering it up.

It really is remarkable, you know, it was all there, the enormity of the formation, just that alone. Then the fact that it had obviously been letters or numbers, you know, a very specific message had been written out and then this whole cover up, I don't doubt that a bit.

Samples of the Kansas crop have been sent for analysis. Of all the reports of crop pictograms that I have received, this is the most intriguing, for the following reasons:

1. The event was preceded by two eyewitness accounts of the same aerial coloured lights.
2. The influx into a small town of various unmarked government vehicles shortly after the event.
3. The setting up of road blocks.
4. The questioning of residents by men in suits and ties.
5. The three large, red hazardous-waste vehicles.
6. The animal-disposal vehicles.
7. The hot wire (electrified fence).
8. The attempted 'discing' and ploughing of the formation.
9. The spreading of shredded crops on the formations.

The analysis of these details points to the following facts. Some official department knew at a very early stage what was in the field. This early information could only have been available through surveillance monitored at a preselected ground area or targeted from a considerable altitude, and because of this the

formations may have been expected. The necessity of
a rapid cover-up required an alert response unit to be
in the target area.

The shapes of the symbols were probably known
before their attempted obliteration – either before
their creation, or immediately after it by means of
high-altitude photography. If this is so, it means
predictable marks can be created on the surface of the
earth by some known agent. They could be a
demonstration of humanly controllable forces or a
liaison demonstration by a superior power.
Whichever way this mystery is viewed, it is
significant.

Centre of symbols looking
north

Symbols beyond hot wire

Two government vehicles on skyline

Shredded crop strewn on symbols

FURTHER CROP ANALYSIS

On 1 January 1991 I received a letter from Dr W.C. Levengood, whose laboratory is located near Detroit, Michigan, USA, explaining that he had just read our first co-authored book *Circular Evidence*. He wrote that there were many interesting questions raised in the book and those of most interest to him related directly to the morphological changes within plants growing in the circles and the subsequent plant development.

Dr Levengood is a biophysicist and his main studies have been concerned with bioelectrochemical energetics in plants and plant-tissue structures. He has obtained a patent for an 'automatic seed analyzer', which is sold worldwide. The operation of the device is based on an electronic system for examining the tissue integrity and membrane breakdown in seeds. In the course of developing this device a special alloy was found which was very sensitive to redox reactions occurring in the developing or germinating of seeds and seedlings. His work on this was published in the peer-reviewed *Journal of Bioelectrochemistry and Bioenergetics*. Also published is his work relating to the effects of electric currents on organelles in plant cells. He has had more than fifty papers published in peer-reviewed journals. His experience covers a wide range of disciplines, many on the study of crops in areas that could relate to the crop-circle phenomenon.

In his letter Dr Levengood pointed out his interest in carrying out the detailed examination of crop seeds and tissue taken from crop circles and comparative control samples taken from the same field. In the case of seeds, he planned to explore the germination characteristics within the material removed from the circle and make comparisons with the normal metabolic cycles of these from the control areas. If he were to discover differences between these samples then they may provide a clue to the form of energy involved in the formation of the circles.

He wrote, 'If some form of electromagnetic energy is involved in the formation of these circles, then (based on what I am finding in recent research) there is a good chance that the intracellular spatial associations between organelles would be quite different in plant tissues from the circle regions than from tissues from the normal growing plants.'

I replied, thanking Dr Levengood for his generous offer of help, and I kept up a supply of circle and control samples from various sites throughout 1991. It is from these samples that the following data has been produced, with one exception. The exception is the very first samples I sent to Dr Levengood, in late January 1991. They were well-preserved circle and control samples I had taken from two formation sites in July 1990. His report, received on 24 February 1991, is historic because it has proved to be the basis of new knowledge, with connotations of unique and exciting avenues of research.

Dr Levengood's report on the sample from circle 'A':

The first cursory view or impression one gets from the seed heads and glumes from within the circles is a situation of normal development. Outwardly the glumes appeared to be filled out to the same degree as the control plants. This did not prove to be the case; all of the glumes from within the circles were empty of seeds. However, this is not the end of the story.

On further examination a condition known as 'polyembryony' was observed in over 90% of the glumes. Polyembryony is an uncommon genetic aberration and is manifested as the formation of multiple embryos within a single glume. The endosperm does not form therefore they are not seeds.

So that I might obtain some perspective of probability of finding seedless heads in a normal field of wheat, I contacted experts in the growing and breeding of wheat at Pro Seed Inc. Michigan for whom I am a consultant. I have two associates there, one an agronomist, the other a plant breeder. Without giving them any details I posed the question, 'What is the probability of randomly removing a single, normal appearing wheathead in a field and finding it completely empty?' In essence their answer was, 'About as likely as winning a lottery three times in a row.'

Report on sample from circle 'B':

Again, all the glumes were devoid of seeds and although the

polyembryony condition was observed, only a very small percentage of the glumes contained the bare embryos. Over 90% of the glumes were completely or embryo free. The difference between the degree of polyembryony formation in circles 'A' and 'B' is readily understood when we consider that they were fifty miles apart, the fields may not have been at the same stage of development and the circles were not formed on the same date.

Report on soil samples 'A' and 'B':

Soil samples taken from outside the circles were more reddish in colour than those from within. This could be a change in the oxidation state of the iron in the soil, a change in the ferrous/ferric ratio. What we need here is the help of a soil chemist.

Dr Levengood concluded his first and most noteworthy report by adding, 'I am finding this a most enjoyable and exciting project.'

A further letter, dated 30 April 1991, contained improved-quality photographs of the normal control seeds and the polyembryo mutations from the first samples.

In the latter part of April 1991 I sent circle and control samples to Dr Levengood that I had taken from the controversial Butleigh Wootton circle, which I had deemed a hoax.

The report was as follows:

Wheat plants and soil samples from Butleigh Wootton received May 2nd. No difference between plant cell structure or soil colours when comparing circle samples with controls.

I then sent samples from the large Newton St Loe pictogram. Dr Levengood reported:

Samples from one of the large circles. Control taken 300m from formation.

Plant cell structure. In the parenchyma cells of the stem nodes the cell wall pits were much more prominent and sharply outlined in the nodes from the circle material than in the control node tissue.

Soil. Colour differences observed. Soil from roots of controls more reddish in colour than from the circle sample.

Seed examination. Externally, the heads and glumes as in other previous samples were of normal appearance. The seeds from both samples were not completely mature. They were white and the endosperm had not completely filled out. About a hundred seeds were obtained from each sample. It was very apparent there were a large number of malformed seeds in the circle sample, about 40% compared to 0% in the controls. These malformations consisted of brown coloured, completely flattened seeds compared to those with the embryo exposed and extending out of one end of the seeds.

Most of these deformations can be explained by a premature dehydration of the seeds. For this to have occurred the development must have been arrested in the circle samples at the time of the pictogram formation. The control plants apparently continued development during the eleven day shipment period. This is the second sample group in which embryo, or seed development has been altered or suppressed.

Dr Levengood also commented on grass and soil samples sent to him by Michael Chorost from a 7.3-metre-diameter ring found at Dandridge, Tennessee:

No obvious differences between plants taken from the ring and those from control.

Soil. The control soil sample was again observed to be more reddish in colour than the samples taken from the ring. A sample taken from the unaffected centre patch was very similar to the control.

Radiation measurements were carried out by Mr Marshall Dudley on the soil samples. A gas flow system was used to make long term counts in these samples. Both beta and alpha particles were monitored in soil from outside the circle, from the centre patch and from the ring. No difference was found in the beta particle counts; however, the alpha particle count from the ring sample was significantly lower than the control. There was no measurable radiation associated with this event.

The lower alpha count suggests there is much more work to be carried out in this discipline.

Dr Levengood has taken special notice of changes in the crop-stem nodes. These are the apparent joints placed at intervals along the stems. The way these are affected when the stems endeavour to recover to the vertical position after being laid down opens up yet another avenue of research. He reported:

During a cursory examination of plant stem samples, there appeared to be an alteration in the growth nodes. The nodes appeared to be thicker on the circle samples than on the control samples.

A ratio method was employed to compare plant stem diameter to node diameter.

N = node diameter.

In = diameter of stem taken 5 mm above node.

R = ratio = N/In.

Each sample consisted of three stems. The stems have five nodes and the bottom node was designated No. 1. Therefore, there were a total three ratio values obtained from each of the five node positions. The mean values of these three ratios were statistically analyzed in the three test samples. It was quite apparent there was no significant difference between these mean values for nodes 1, 4 and 5. In nodes 2 and 3 the nodes were significantly different as shown.

Samples were of stems from a circle with an outer ring.

Sample	Ratio N/In	Standard deviation	Confidence level
A-Circle	1.434	0.082	P<0.05 (significant)
B-Ring	1.354	0.077	P<0.05 (significant)
C-Control	1.242	0.085	....

Microscopic Examination: *Detailed comparisons of the node tissue in samples A, B and C disclosed some very interesting differences in cell structure and opened up another exciting perspective in these studies. In both A and B node tissues, the accentuated cell wall pit formations were again seen as I described in an August report. If you compare photo marked 'Node 3 Control' with photo marked 'Node 3 Circle', you will note many small, well outlined cell wall pits in the circle tissue (arrow shows an example). Also compare node 4 control and sample where the*

differences are again seen, however, in this case the cell wall pits are slightly elongated.

It appears that some mechanism has expanded and increased the diameter of these pits. An indication of this cell wall stretching is shown in the photo marked 'Node 2 Circle' [not included – P.D.] where faint lines are extending out from the pits. What appears to have occurred is a rapid expansion of the pit structures. Also from the accumulating data there is some indication that the greater the node size ratio the more expanded are the cell wall pits.

Visual seed examination by Dr Levengood revealed the following percentages of abnormal seeds:

Sample	Abnormal Seeds
A-Circle	32.3%
B-Ring	10.0%
C-Control	1.2%

ALTON BARNES

Sample	Abnormal seeds
D-Circle	20.0%
E-Control	1.5%

MAISEY FARM

Sample	Abnormal seeds
H-Ring	6.3%
I-Control	1.0%

ALTON PRIORS

Sample	Abnormal seeds
Circle Floor	11.0%
Control	1.0%

STONEHENGE

Sample	Abnormal seeds
Circle Floor	6.7%
Control	1.3%

LOCKERIDGE

Sample	Abnormal seeds
Oval Floor	0.0%
Control	0.6%

Dr Levengood adds: 'In this last sample [Lockeridge] the plants were close to maturity when the formation appeared and may account for the lack of abnormal seeds.'

(Comment by P.D.: From a site in Cornwall, Jill Harris sent me some samples of grass she had taken from a small field known as Carn Marth at Carharrack. The samples were from an area that had been flattened to form a 12-metre-diameter ring with a 'Y' shape inside it. The arms of the 'Y' were equidistant from each other and about 0.7 metre wide. Black substance was found on the flattened grass only at the junction of the arms to the ring. Samples were sent from these areas as well as from other parts of the ring. No control sample was sent to me.)

Dr Levengood reported:

Grass samples received July 15th. The grass blades were coated with a dead black (non light reflecting) substance. This substance was very uniformly spread on the blades but was easily removed by rubbing with the fingers and felt greasy. The dead grass taken from other points in the ring did not show this coating material.

A microscopic examination revealed no hyphae or mycelium thus reducing the possibility of fungi. This material was amorphous in appearance and was very suggestive of carbon black. The underlying leaf cells had completely broken-down cell walls with large gaps in them. There was no regularity in the cell outlines as was seen in the comparison tissue taken from other locations along the ring. Any other work on this should involve a spectrophotometric analysis to determine the composition of the amorphous substance.

(Comment by P.D.: While investigating the Alton Priors pictogram this year I noticed four areas of the flattened crop had a black substance attached only to the upper surfaces. On close examination I could see that if I moved the affected plant some of the substance fell off, appearing to be light and flaky. On other areas it remained firmly attached as though smeared on to the surface.

Under a magnifying glass at home, I could see a clear solidified bubble integrated with some of the flakes, which reminded me of charred pine wood.)

The following report concerns the samples I sent to Dr Levengood:

Microscopic Examination: *The intact wheat heads were observed to have patches of this black material over what is presumed to be the upper surfaces and located in most cases at the upper or bearded end of the seed glume. It was quite apparent that the black regions were where the plant tissue had been severely 'charred'. In fact, fragments of this charred tissue still retained the cell structure on a macro scale (40x mag.). Many loose charred fibres had broken away and were scattered over the surface of the seed heads. In several regions fibres were located which were still attached to the seed beard and occasionally only the tip of a fibre had been charred. There are no indications of any external 'substance' having been applied to the plants.*

This charred tissue is however a very interesting effect and for it to have occurred in the form seen here, the following conditions were necessary:

1. The plant tissue must have been on the dry side. This was confirmed by the fact that the control seeds were very close to harvest maturity, therefore the plant stalks and outer tissue of the seed heads would not be green and hydrated.

2. For carbonization of this nature, the heating must have been in a reducing (non-oxidizing) atmosphere.

3. The heating must have been intense and for a very brief period, otherwise underlying tissue would have been charred.

At this juncture I again examined the grass samples previously discussed. In this tissue the black layer appeared to have been applied to the leaves in a very uniform layer.

On re-examination it became evident that the black layer was really composed of the charred suberized layer on the leaf surface. This is a waxy film which would, under reducing conditions, become amorphous carbon. I would say that both of these samples were produced under very similar conditions as outlined above. In fact, the energies might be quite similar in all of these formations, they only appear different because as the crop matures changes take place in the plant's response and sensitivity to the imparted energy.

Thanks to Dr Levengood's generosity in time and effort in producing these reports, the research on plant and soil samples extracted from crop formations has taken a massive step forward.

I wrote to Dr Levengood in September 1991, seeking his views on the following proposal. It occurs to me that it would be very useful if a crop-analysis programme could be set up with the following parameters. As soon as a crop circle appears in a field that has also suffered wind damage, a medium-sized man-made circle should be constructed in the same field. From these three sources – wind damage, the man-made circle and the circle under investigation – regular periodic samples, say weekly, could be taken and compared by analysis with control samples, as in the chart on the facing page.

This kind of monitoring would establish hitherto unknown growth anomalies such as the behaviour of stem nodes and seed abnormalities.

Of course, the perfect situation would be an on-site mobile laboratory, as this would, among many other things, eliminate transport delays.

SAMPLE FROM

SAMPLE TAKEN END OF
WEEK 1
WEEK 2
WEEK 3
WEEK 4
WEEK 5

CONTROL:

WIND DAMAGE:

MAN-MADE CIRCLE:

CIRCLE:

Normal cell structure

Expanded cell-wall pits

Normal cell structure

Elongated cell-wall pits

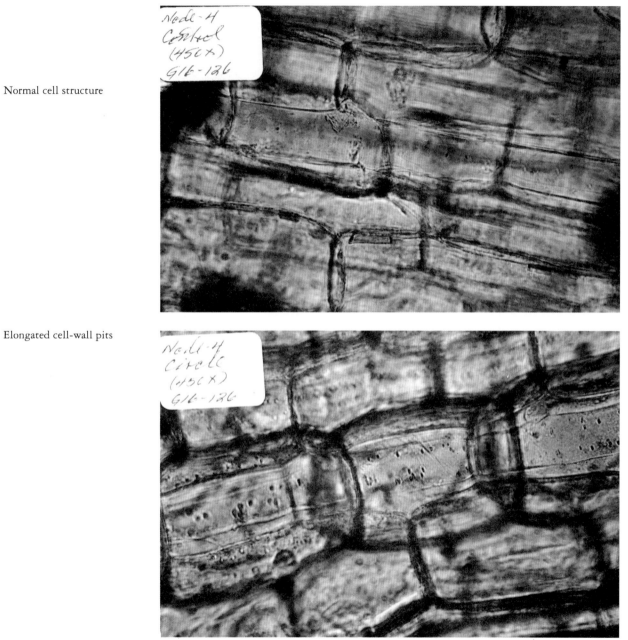

HOLY PLACES AND CROP CIRCLES

Temples and churches are built by man. Those who help with their construction are aware of the special purpose of their labours and consequently their minds are tuned, albeit subconsciously, in such a way as to immerse the structure in a special atmosphere or energy field. Being a structure, it will acquire its own pattern of energy, drawn from and influenced by those around it. Being a place of worship and reverence, its energy field will increase and consolidate through its location and those who visit it, and thus it will acquire its individuality.

Those who enter this building, not knowing who built it or how it was built, will have certain sensitivities increased by the knowledge that they are in a special place. How many people walk into a church and sense an atmosphere? This, coupled with a certain amount of random expectancy, will blend their energy pattern with that of the building. The result of this blending is that people will become able to describe their individual emotions, and because we are dealing with temples and churches, these emotions vary very little from peace, love and unity. In fact they are what you want them to be, although what the building represents to you also has an influence.

A crop circle is a structure of a kind and, as such, energy criteria similar to those in temples and churches will apply, but this time it is something special and unique. In comparison to a church, the crop circle's material, shape and location enhance the sensitivities more and consequently will usually have a greater impact on your emotions, which are also influenced by what you think the circle represents.

This hypothesis is illustrated by the following incident. While driving along the A272 southeast of Winchester, I noticed a lady standing some distance out in a field of wheat and staring straight ahead. Being familiar with the locations of crop circles in that area, I knew there were none in that particular field, so I stopped to see what she had found. I got out of the car and stood on the grass bank overlooking the field. I watched her raising and lowering her hands in a gentle motion and periodically moving to another position, all of which I recognized as bare-hands dowsing. I was fascinated by her concentration but I could not understand why she was so interested in patches of what I knew to be wind-damaged crop. I called to her and she walked through the crop towards me. Her clothes were saturated, owing to earlier rain.

I said I could see she was dowsing and asked if she had found anything of interest. She said some of the circles had energy patterns and there were two ley lines passing across them. With some diplomacy I explained that it was wind damage she had been dowsing, and told her how such features can be recognized. It is important to note that she had discovered what she considered to be impressive energy patterns in a crop circle, not knowing it was wind damage; a classic case of finding patterns simply because that is what you are expecting to find.

It is a fact that the mind can be dominated by expectancy. I once entered a circle which I knew to be a hoax. There were two people already in it and they were dowsing with rods and describing to each other the sensations they were experiencing. We began talking and they told me about the energies they had felt as they were approaching the circle and how these energies became stronger as they entered. They also described the warmth and peace that permeated the area. I thought, how wonderful that man can create such a place as this and unknowingly have created what may be termed a shrine. Does it really matter how circles are created if this is the effect they can produce? The inseparability of cause and effect was never better demonstrated.

There is no guarantee that the energies found in a circle considered to be genuine will be any different from those found in a hoax circle. Emotional energies can be found in areas such as man-made circles and even patches of wind-damaged crop. If you desire your emotional and detection sensitivities to be enhanced, they will be. If you and the place feel right, whether it is a holy place or an area of flattened crop, then you already have the only requirements. I am sure there are some people who feel closer to their God or more spiritually aware in a crop circle than they do in a conventional place of worship.

I have always maintained that this avenue of thought highlights the unique energy characteristics of each crop circle. Just as we have unique fingerprints, so the crop circles have unique energy prints. They are the reason for the increasing number of people who are becoming spiritually aware. I am sure the world is already a better place for the way we have reacted to crop circles, despite the short time they have been significant.

May the parallels between holy places and crop circles long continue, for no one can criticize their benefits of love and unity.

THE PRESENT SITUATION

More circles, more pictograms, more people involved, more groups, more meetings, more theories, more research, more published articles, more books, more stories, more intrigue and more mystery. That about sums up the present state of the continuing crop-circle phenomenon. When you think about it, nothing much has changed – only the scale of each of the above categories. All the evidence I have logged indicates what I would have expected: steady increases in each.

The single circle, of course, cannot change except in its floor patterning. It will always be the basic shape to which everything else is referred, as though it is the heart of the subject. I am constantly reminded by the thoughts of many people who contact me, that the single circle has a unique magic of its own. All the thoughts, the dreams and visions can be found there while you are contemplating a circle, whether on your own or with friends. Time resolutely passes but the hidden enigmatic mystery of the single crop circle seems to be timeless. However it is created, it is a symbol of your own desires. From it can be extracted a range of emotions, as well as progress towards an inner awareness and the knowledge that countless others have already benefited or will benefit from a similar experience.

Pictograms are a different matter. In many cases, it seems to me, a foundation constant can be found in the shapes and groups; a hallmark, maybe even a signature. I am sure the pictograms emphasize whatever is uppermost in our minds and as they are a feature on the earth itself, our thoughts often turn to environmental issues. It is a well-known fact that our planet is troubled by man-made pollution, and consequently many people see the formations as a sign of caution, reading them as valid messages about the dangerously high levels of toxic waste we discharge into our atmosphere and seas and rivers. This insight is endorsed by the Hopi Indians of North America, intelligent people who are probably one of the few remaining races on Earth who understand it for what it really is, a living organism. They are very worried about the planet and the way it is deteriorating, perhaps beyond the point of no return. They see the crop circles as a cry for help and I am sure there is no more valid reason for their existence.

If the intelligence behind the pictograms forms part of an overall supreme intelligence, then of course the individual characteristics of this part of the whole would be displayed. In this way, interest is maintained in the phenomenon at an ideal level for whatever the original purpose may have been. As I have said many times, if that purpose is to increase unity among people, then it certainly has been successful.

Many people have a favourite pictogram. For them that individual pattern may portray their spiritual characteristics. Through the acceptable medium of flattened crops, it provides a focal point for meditation, something they may not have experienced before. I have seen people gazing for long periods into a pictogram and, with some measure of serendipity, I am sure the results were beneficial. This situation can be likened to the fractal basis of the Mandelbrot Set, whereby your thoughts magnify the sequential fronds of knowledge, perhaps on an infinite journey of discovery.

More and more people have become associated in some way with crop circles in recent years. The exponential escalation can be attributed to the subject itself, which continues to be a mystery without a possible solution in sight. Many ask how it is that despite the number of people involved, we seem to have made such little progress. The answer depends on where you are looking and what kind of information you seek, in which direction you are focusing your enquiry. This is where the phenomenon could be portraying its main purpose. It caters for the individualism of people, allowing their personal characteristics to define the avenues to be explored. Their voyages of discovery, like the spokes of a wheel, lead to the hub where lies the universal consciousness. This is a specific spiritual advance.

It must be added that an advance in one specific scientific direction has produced significant revelations. It is those made by Dr Levengood in his research on plants and soil taken from crop circles but, as he admits, there still remains an enormous amount of work to be done. There is no reason why discoveries by orthodox physics should not complement those made through spiritual avenues. Why should there not be a new level of physio-spiritual integration? It would come under the heading of progress.

I am privileged to be in the position of receiving inputs from both realms and this is why I am able to describe with such conviction the rate of advance of these two approaches. The unseen spiritual unity of many thousands of people through the medium of crop circles must be the envy of many leaders of our society. It also demonstrates the desire to seek and share knowledge about the mysteries underlying even the smallest crop circle, as can be verified by the growth of crop-circle groups in many countries. The old adage 'everyone loves a mystery' has never seemed truer.

The number of members in the groups range from two or three to two or three hundred. Some join just to keep abreast of events, while others are anxious to be included in 'field activities'. As is demonstrated in this book, many people have generously shared the results of their own activities. It is with regret that all cannot be included.

Groups are the backbone of the investigation of crop circles, simply because of the huge areas of countryside that have to be monitored and checked. Each group seems to have its own individual seek, check and record framework and all are apparently working well. The reports, which must now be in their thousands, are all historically important.

Theories about how and why crop circles and pictograms are created continue to be discussed but in a different vein from in previous years. What occurs now when investigating a formation is something that is not as superficial as before. The emphasis is on how neither a vortex nor human manipulation could have created certain features. Of course there is more expertise around now. Many people have seen many circles, and discussions of sound recording, video enhancement and photographic techniques can be quite educational. Encouragingly, much more high technology has been brought to bear on the subject. It means this phenomenon has gained the attention of a larger spectrum of scientists, broadening the overall view.

I hope the analytical results from crop and soil biochemists, electromagnetic engineers, computer operators, radiation technicians, physicists, geographers, meteorologists, phytogenesists and others, as well as the contribution of all those wonderful people who just sit and think, will eventually bring about the final understanding of this mystery. What form it will take, only time will tell, but I am sure it will be most enlightening and a great lesson learned in the name of science.

One thing is for sure: the world has benefited socially and spiritually from all that has flowed so far from this phenomenon. May this trend continue because the need for peace, love, unity and care for our planet was never greater.

Middlesbrough

Ripon

York

Bradford
Leeds

Doncaster

Grimsby

Lincoln

Nottingham

Leicester

Peterborough

Birmingham

Northampton

Cambridge

Hereford

Ipswich

Clacton

Swindon

Amersham
London

Bristol
Bath
Marlborough

Devizes

Wells

Winchester

Ashford

Salisbury

Brighton

Exeter

Swanage

Arreton

Plymouth

Penzance

O = Crop circle or formation